7 STEPS TO EXPORT AND EXPORT BROKERING

THE FAST TRACK GUIDE AND 7-STEPS TO EXPORT SUCCESS

HOW YOU CAN SUCCESSFULLY BROKER DEALS IN THE INTERNATIONAL TRADE (REAL-LIFE EXAMPLES INSIDE)

Mike Wilson & Ramzi Bouchrit

Mike Wilson & Ramzi Bouchrit

Copyright ©2022 Mike Wilson & Ramzi Bouchrit
All Rights Reserved

Cover Design By:

Yassine Essghaier

Contributors:

Mike Wilson from Go Exporting

Ramzi Bouchrit from RB JV Group

7 STEPS TO EXPORT SUCCESS AND EXPORT BROKERING

TABLE OF CONTENTS

INTRODUCTION	5
GO EXPORTING THE 7-STEPS TO EXPORT SUCCESS	7
THE 7-STEPS TO EXPORT SUCCESS	9
STEP ONE – WHY?	9
STEP TWO – WHERE?	10
STEP THREE – HOW?	10
STEP 4 – WHAT NOW?	11
STEP 5 – PREPARE & GO	11
STEP 6 – PERFECT EXECUTION	12
STEP 7 – GROW OR SLOW	13
STEP ONE – WHY?	15
DOES EXPORTING FIT WITH YOUR BUSINESS STRATEGY?	15
EXPORT READINESS	18
ATTITUDE TO RISK	23
STEP TWO – WHERE?	25
LOOK IN-HOUSE	26
WHERE YOUR COMPETITORS SELL?	28
MARKET SIZE DATA	30
CUSTOMER ANALYSIS	31
BARRIERS TO ENTRY	33
CURRENCY	37
COUNTRY RISK	39
CONSOLIDATE & RATE	41
STEP 3 – HOW?	43
DISTRIBUTORS AND AGENTS	45
RECRUITMENT	51
DISTRIBUTOR VERSUS RECRUIT?	53
DIRECT SALES	55
TIME TO COMMIT	57
STEP 4 – WHAT NOW?	61
INSIDE RESOURCE?	65
OUTSIDE RESOURCE	67
STEP 5 - PREPARE & GO	71
VALUE PROPOSITION	74
FIRST STEPS	76
MARKETING	81

THE VISIT	83
ASSESS AND APPOINT	87
REVIEW	90
STEP 6 – PERFECT EXECUTION	93
COMPLETE THE JOB	95
THE CATAPULT	98
STEP 7 – GROW OR SLOW?	103
FOREWORD	107
WHY EXPORT?	111
METHODS OF PAYMENT	117
EXPORT TERMINOLOGIES	127
EXPORT DOCUMENTS	135
HOW TO MAKE AN EXPORT CONTRACT ENFORCEABLE	141
EXPORT BROKERING TIPS	147
HOW TO GET PAID AND FROM WHO	147
HOW TO SECURE OUR FEES AND WHICH MEANS TO USE	149
WHAT TO LOOK FOR AND AVOID IN ANY DEAL (MOSTLY IT'S ABOUT THE BUSINESS PARTNERS):	152
REAL LIFE CASE STUDIES	157
HOW TO LEVERAGE YOUR NETWORK OF LOCAL IMPORTERS AND INCREASE YOUR BOTTOM SALES WITH NO EXTRA COSTS:	157
HOW WE'VE DONE IT STEP BY STEP:	158
TIMBER DEALS TO VIETNAM	160
STEP BY STEP	161
HOW TO ADAPT QUICKLY ACCORDING TO CIRCUMSTANCES:	163
STEP BY STEP:	163
SOYA BEAN DEALS TO CHINA	165
STEP BY STEP:	166
METALS	168
STEP BY STEP:	168
THANK YOU	173

Mike Wilson & Ramzi Bouchrit

Introduction

The FastTrack Guide & 7-Steps to Export Success

How to Get Started Fast, Avoid the Pitfalls and be on your way to Export Success

Congratulations on taking the first step in starting or increasing your sales in international markets. It can be a scary prospect and often where to start to get things going is the hardest part!

You are now part of the 10% club. Only 1 in 10 SMEs export, with the majority stating the reasons as fear of the unknown, lack of internal skills, resources or capacity. Identifying that you may need some support and guidance is the fundamental key to success.

Follow a few simple guidelines and exporting can be easier than you think. It will bring real, tangible rewards to your business. On average SMEs add £300k of sales through export. This guide will take you through the 7-Steps to be well on your way to £1m!

Our FastTrack system will give you a framework to work with; from deciding whether you are ready to export, finding where the opportunities lie, through to making the first sales and growing your international business.

We'll show you how to plan and develop your market entry strategy, what pitfalls and dangers to look out for along the way, and the simple tools we use to bring export success.

The FastTrack approach has been developed out of the experience gained in over 30 years' travelling the world to open and expand international markets, generating $2b+ in revenues along the way for start-ups, SMEs and multi-national corporates.

I've not only built up 1000's of air miles, worn out several suitcases and been close to both man-made and natural disasters, from terrorism to ash clouds, but also worked out the hard way the 7 key steps required to be successful.

No one instinctively knows how to sell in international markets, it's different in virtually every country for one thing. But armed with the right strategy, coupled with the flexibility to react to ever changing circumstance, it can be a fun journey with clear benefits to your business.

There are no short cuts, but that does not mean success has to be slow. I used the 7 steps in this book to go from zero to £1m in sales inside 12 months in one country alone. The quicker you complete each step the faster results will be achieved.

BUT miss a step or don't complete it thoroughly enough and danger lurks around the corner! Don't be tempted to rush in and ideally seek the advice and support of an experienced mentor along the journey.

So, you've not been put off by my preamble and have decided exporting is the way forward for your business? You want to know about how to FastTrack your business through the 7 Steps Checklist to £1m in sales?

Sounds good and you are hopefully excited about setting out on this journey.

Let's get into it then by first of all summarising the 7-Steps. The framework and stages you need to go through to develop and implement your export strategy. A more detailed description of each stage follows in the subsequent pages.

**Mike Wilson
Go Exporting**

The 7-Steps to Export Success

Step One – Why?
Before anything else you need to be clear why you want to export and whether your organisation is ready for the challenge. We will explore:
- Your motivations to export
- What you are looking to achieve, over what period
- Your attitude to risk
- The resources you can allocate and the timeframe
- Your organisational readiness, is everyone on board?
- Will exporting affect your current business?
- How to assess these factors and decide your next move

Step Two – Where?

You've decided that exporting is right for you at this time, so where do you start? How do you identify and assess the best markets? We will discuss:

- Assessing your in-house data
- How to learn from your competitors
- Market research
- Evaluating the market potential
- Who are your customers?
- Barriers to Entry
- Risks
- How to evaluate these factors to rate the different potential markets and decide on your key target priorities

Step Three – How?

We now have our target market(s), so the next critical step is deciding how we are going to reach the market and carve out a share of the business?

- How to decide how many market(s) your organisation is ready to enter
- Where to focus

- Which route to market to choose; distributor, agent, recruitment, direct, online etc.
- Forming a detailed plan, what to consider
- Setting milestones and expected outcomes to benchmark progress
- Stakeholder buy-in

Step 4 – What Now?

In this step we look at how to implement your plan. A nice strategy is all well and good but it needs a clear plan of action too.

- The importance of focus
- Deciding who is best to lead the charge
- Assessing your internal resource
- Benefits of external support
- Avoid 'Touch & Go' selling

Step 5 – Prepare & Go

Now you know who and how you will implement your strategy, make sure everything is ready to go to market, to receive those first orders

- Preparation – make sure your organisation is ready

- What is your Value Proposition?
- How to take your first steps in the market
- What are the best marketing methods?
- Making your first country visit
- Review and Appoint your partners/staff
- Review progress versus your milestones and targets

Step 6 – Perfect Execution

The first orders are received, job done? It's really just beginning! Here we look at the importance of getting it right the first time and building upon your success.

- Ensure 100% customer satisfaction
- Deal with any issues fast
- How to ask for repeat orders
- Understanding your customers buying cycle
- Building references and case studies
- Asking the 'often forgotten' questions
- Building upon your success, the Catapult

Step 7 – Grow or Slow

You are now 6-12 months in to your journey. Everything is going well and you are even considering expanding in the market. Wait!

- Take a breath and review
- Check those Milestones and Targets
- Assess your progress in detail
- Evaluate if you are making money
- Reassess your strategy and planning
- Review risks versus rewards of expansion
- How fast and how far should you go?
- Develop a new Stage 2 plan with new Milestones & Targets
- Agree with all stakeholders

7 Steps to Export Success And Export Brokering

STEP ONE – WHY?

Before going any further and committing resources to exporting, take a step back, ask yourself why?
- Why do you want to export?
- What started you thinking about embarking on this journey?

Perhaps growth has slowed in your home market and you see the next opportunity overseas? Maybe your competitors are exporting and you want to get in on the act? It could be you have started receiving enquiries and even orders without knowing why or how?

These are all good reasons for thinking about exporting, but before you take the plunge you need to do a bit of soul searching and self-assessment.

Does Exporting fit with your business strategy?

What is your true motivation? It's no good thinking I can export to so and so country and maybe I'll get a few sales.

More than likely, the time and effort involved will not be worth the return.

It is important that exporting fits in to your overall strategy for your company. Perhaps your objective is to double the size of the business within 5 years for example. A nice goal for sure, but without careful planning and consideration, is it really realistic? Perhaps it may even be too cautious!

The first task therefore is to consider whether exporting fits in with the overall strategy of your company. Go back to your business plan, your mission statement if you have one, think about what you set out to achieve with your business. Was exporting part of that plan? Is it an integral part of your thinking?

The point is you need information on which to base your decisions.

Wanting to do something is all well and good, but do you have the wherewithal to actually do it? I'd love to play in the British Open Golf Tournament but unfortunately, I do not have the skills required, although sometimes I kid myself I have!

Take a long hard look at yourself and your organisation. Self-awareness is critical at this early stage. Beware embarking on export as a vanity project, where you think it will look good for your image and give you the chance to travel on the company! If you just like the idea of travelling and showing pins on a map, then it is really time to take a step back. Exporting requires commitment of time and resources. It's not an easy ride.

Business travel is hard, it is expensive and a thief of time. I wish I had a £1 for every minute I've spent in the air or at an airport, sat in a hotel or in a car.

So, before going any further, think about why you want to export and what you want to achieve. Write it down, then go off and do something else, before looking at the list again tomorrow. Does it still make sense?!

Is export right for you at this stage in your business?

Even if it was not written down or a conscious ambition, is export a logical outcome from your plans for growth for example? Analyse all of this and be clear in your mind that exporting is a strategic choice which matches the ambitions of your organisation.

If the result of this analysis is yes, we want to export, then the next step is to make a list of the reasons why you want to export and what you want to achieve.

Write it down, be as honest and clear as possible. Then go off and do something else, leave it overnight, before coming back to it and reviewing again.

Does it still make sense? Are you committed? Is exporting right for your business at this stage in your development? Be certain before committing further time and resources.

Export Readiness

Assuming you have completed the two tasks above and are happy that your motivations for exporting are legitimate and match your business strategy, the next task is to assess if your organisation is also ready.

Are all the stakeholders in the business of the same opinion and ready for the challenge? It is important to be certain of this, to get their commitment and make sure everyone is on the same page. Better to find any dissenters now than further down the line. This may seem obvious, but it is not always the case. Ask the question, get commitment from all involved, make sure everyone is on the same page.

This will be doubly important later if things are not quite going to plan and you need extra support.

Make a list of the resources you are going to need to start exporting and the potential internal barriers to success. Next compare that with the organisation's actual current capabilities. Look at your staff, do they have the required skills and experience? Are your products, packaging and marketing material export ready? Start off looking at the people in your company, in every department that will be affected by exporting, so that means every department!

Do they have the skills and experience required for exporting? If not what training or re-organisation is required to meet that need. Make sure the whole organisation is aware of your plans and ask each department to prepare accordingly. It may take some time, so start early.

If you are already exporting to other areas then likely you have the skills in place, that's great, but you still need to go through the process to ensure the organisation can cope with the likely extra demands of any new market. Remember each country is different.

For example, if your product needs local approval it could be that you require specific packaging, labelling and paperwork for each country. That could take some time to prepare and may have unexpected consequences. It is best to discuss internally to be sure there are no unforeseen obstacles to considering a new market.

I worked with one company who had product approval in France, for example. Their packaging process was highly automated with reels of pre-printed sheets which were then formed around the product. Each reel contained packaging for 50,000 units, but in the early stages sales were unknown and likely to be no more than 10,000 units in Year 1. An internal decision was required to make the required investment ahead of potential sales.

It's the classic chicken and egg situation. You have to be sure in advance that your organisation is prepared to and able to make the investment.

One key resource which needs to be taken into account is **finance**. It is often overlooked in the flush of expectation, but exporting has financial consequences for your company. Yes, it will bring a real benefit and cash generation later on, but in the early stages it will be a draw on your cashflow.

The initial research, travel to the market, marketing, internal costs, cashflow consequences etc etc will all be on your FDs mind. Best therefore to discuss in advance. Agree how much you are willing to invest and the length of time you are able to continue before expected returns kick in.

Go Exporting offers its clients an audit of their business readiness to export, including a ready-made checklist template for assessing your resources. This checklist can be found in Appendix One/Below

7 Steps to Export Success And Export Brokering

Go Exporting 7-Steps to Export Success - Resources Checklist

Resource	In-Place/Known	Needs Improving	Not Currently Available	Action Required/comments
People Knowledge & Availability Export Customs Procedures International Payments International Sales International Marketing Foreign Language Cultural Understanding Business Methods Understanding International Standards & Approvals Specialist Export Sales person(s) Internal Sales Support Customer Service Support International Freight/Shipping/Incoterms International VAT requirements Duty/Tariffs Packaging & Labelling Product Development for Export Customer training capability (if required)				
Product Suitable for export? Approvals in place? What is the product origin? Sufficient stock? Export packaging available				
Production Available capacity? Raw material availability Sufficient production staff for export? QC & Testing capability Acceptable lead times for export				
Finance Cashflow to cover export investment Attitude to risk matches export plans Multiple currency capability International payment facilities Expertise to manage currency fluctuations Credit insurance in place Documentation in multiple languages				
Sales Dedicated export person/team? International sales agreements incl distribution/agents				
Marketing Collateral in foreign languages? E.g. brochures, flyers Customer documents in multiple languages e.g. manuals Capability to plan international campaign Social media accounts in multiple/target countries				

Attitude to Risk

As part of this debate it is important to also define your organisations attitude to risk. Inevitably there will be some additional exposure, not just financially, but also legally, politically, even environmentally perhaps.

Entering a new country there may well be an element of the unknown. Even within Europe there are differences country to country. Get it wrong and it can be costly. Be aware of the pitfalls and if in doubt ask advice.

As an example, I worked with an organisation looking to appoint an agent in Germany. Sounds straightforward right? Well yes and no. Appointing one and drawing up a simple contract is easy enough, but there are unforeseen consequences under European law. An agent could actually be entitled to part of the increase in value of your business in that country as compensation if your agreement ever ends. They could also be viewed as an employee if the contract is not written correctly.

The moral of the story is to get advice before you act, even if you think it should be straightforward.

It is important to understand your attitude to risk and agree the level of investment you are prepared to make.

What timeframe are you prepared to commit to?

How long are you prepared/are you able to be exposed to risk?

Will an export campaign affect the rest of your business?

Do you need outside support and what will it cost?

It is important to not only consider the financial risk but also the legal, political and perhaps even environmental factors which could affect the success of your business.

I've worked with more than one organisation who, when we've really analysed their business and motivations together, have realised the timing is not quite right for them to start exporting now.

If that is the case, we agree the conditions that need to apply before reconsidering and look to how we can work towards achieving them.

More often than not, after a period of time they are ready and able to successfully export and we start with Step 2 of the '7 Steps' programme.

STEP TWO – WHERE?

So now you understand why you want to export and what you want to achieve within the limitations of your organisation and the resources available to you.

What next? Where to start? There are 195 recognised countries in the world, so you certainly cannot be everywhere at once, no matter what the size of your company! Even Coca Cola is not everywhere. There are actually 2 countries they do not officially sell to for political reasons.

How do you narrow down and identify your target market? Gut instinct? **NO!**

Well in truth, you can probably already narrow this down considerably from your existing knowledge and logic on the potential size of the market in each area. The U.S.A. is bound to have bigger potential than Papua New Guinea for example. Yet at the same time it may have more competitors and barriers to entry. Sometimes it is also more profitable to be a bigger fish in a smaller pond.

Nevertheless, you need to take a much more measured and scientific approach than that, really get to know the possibilities for your product or service, decide which will be your target market; or markets, depending on the results of your self-awareness assessment in STEP ONE.

Look in-house.

Research your own data. Where do your enquiries come from? Where do you sell at the moment? Do you understand why? What are the drivers for those customers to buy from you? Is it a one off or is there a real market demand? Ask them for feedback.

You hopefully have some form of CRM system or database; if not, start using one immediately to capture contacts, enquiries, build a database of target companies.

There are very good cloud-based options out there, which are often free initially depending on number of users. Agile and Hubspot are good options which I find very useful and easy to use, with lots of scaleable options as you grow.

Take note however of the new GDPR regulations to ensure you stay on the correct side of data protection.

Assuming you have in-house data, this should give you a pointer to where overseas interest for your product/service may lie. Do you receive multiple enquiries from one particular area? Do you have a record of what has created the interest when you have followed up?

This is important and may provide some eye opening, unexpected potential target markets.

For example, when working with one organisation we noted a number of enquiries coming in from Qatar. Now, although we were active in the region, Qatar was not a particular focus, so to suddenly receive quality enquiries was a surprise.

Looking into it further we found that, due to political tensions in the region, other Gulf states had closed borders with Qatar, so stopping cross region trade. Companies in the country were therefore urgently looking for alternative suppliers. The team jumped on this opportunity and turned it in to good business.

What about your existing customers? Are you selling to any particular countries right now? Again, this can be an important indicator of a market opportunity. It is important to understand why they are buying from you. What created the demand in the first place? What is it about your product or service which makes it attractive to them? Understand whether this was a once off requirement or something they need on a regular basis.

Ask the questions and often you will find the answers. Gather feedback from your customers.

Where your competitors sell?

You've looked at where your enquiries come from and where you currently sell to, which is a good start as a guide. But if you are new, you may not have this information to call upon. So, what next?

One simple option is to look at your competitors. Often, they can be a great guide as to where the good markets are. Get to know them as well as you can. Research them on the internet, look for news stories on their website, tweets or other social media posts. Speak to their team when you meet them, you'll be surprised how people like to talk and what you can learn.

Beware however as they may be trying to do the same to you, so be careful what you say!

Look at where your competitors have their own sales team or a distributor/agent. Have they been present in that country for a number of years? Do they have a subsidiary? This will give you a prime insight in to where they see the market.

Look further into the competitor's marketing. Where do they advertise? Do they produce brochures in a certain language? Which conferences and exhibitions do they attend?

Next check out where they have specific product approvals if relevant to your product/service. Are they a member of any overseas trade bodies? They probably will not have made this investment if they do not see a market potential.

Put all the bits of information together and it will give you an indication of potential target markets.

Don't worry that the competitors are present in a market before you. That will often be the case, there are always competitors. It shows you there is a market for your product/service and, providing you are confident in the value proposition of your product, there is no reason why you cannot take a share of the market.

Get to know your competitors better than ever before. They may well save you a lot of time, money and effort by pointing you in the right direction.

Market Size Data

Competitors and in-house data are helpful, but what if they are misleading? The question is how big is the potential? Is there any real data on the market size?

In an ideal world there would be official data on the size of market for your product/service in your target country. It's worth checking with Government departments, Chambers of Commerce and trade bodies first just in case.

Unfortunately, however, it is rarely the case, so we have to look to other sources. There are many private research companies out there who compile data on a particular market sector and offer it for sale on sites such as MarketResearch.com. These can be pricey and may not be exactly what you are looking for however.

Another alternative is to commission you own research through a Market Research company. This again can be very expensive as it involves dedicated resource on your specific project for a period of time. It may well provide a very detailed report however with a lot of useful data. From experience it is rare clients go to this expense or even require this level of detail.

The other alternative is to use a consultant such as [Go Exporting](#) who often offer cost-effective, targeted research packages, designed from experience to give the right level of information when considering entering a new market. Often these are offered at a competitive cost in order to build a relationship with clients and introduce further services in the future.

International trade data can also be gathered from organisations such as the International Trade Centre, Zauba and private companies specialising in this field like Quevedos.

Customer Analysis

We've already looked at where you and your competition's existing customers are, but we also need to analyse whether the buyer for your products or service is the same in each market.

Sounds obvious right? Well no, there can be subtle differences in each country's usual practice and supply chain set up which you really need to take in to account.

It can make a big difference to your best route to market and may bring about different obstacles, or barriers to entry, which need to be considered.

Is there a different supply chain set up? Are there specifies involved? Does the government or ultimate client purchase directly, or do subcontractors procure as part of an overall package or service? The distinctions may seem slight, but it can make a big difference to the ease of market entry and therefore the market potential.

As an example, one company I worked with supplied its product usually to contractors who carried out work on behalf of the client. The client purchased a complete service including material from the contractor.

To be successful it was necessary to not only persuade the contractor to buy, but also to work with the client on specifications to ensure the product was high on the list of options to the contractor.

In the U.S.A. however the client, in this case the Local Government, purchases the material directly and free issues it to the contractor. Typically, they give out large annual or bi-annual tenders to approved suppliers.

In this instance all the sales focus is on the client, as the contractor has little influence over the choice of product. Price also becomes very important in this scenario. Once suppliers are on the approved list it is assumed their products are equal, hence differentiation is mostly on price.

Even with consumer products there can be differences in route to market, for example do you need to go through wholesalers or direct to the retailers? In this instance the size of your sales team will be different in each scenario.

Be sure you know the route to market in your target market in order to be able to devise your strategy correctly.

Barriers to Entry

So, we've identified what appears to be a lucrative country for our products. There is a good market size and we have identified who the potential customers are. All seems good, but we are not yet ready to commit. First, we must identify the barriers to entry.

Every market has these, most are surmountable as long as you are aware of them, but others can delay or even make the project not worthwhile. Some are official and others just common practice, but nonetheless effective barriers.

Firstly, are there official approvals required before you can sell? Is there a national certification or government registration process? If there is, will they accept approval from another country as proof of meeting the required criteria? This can save a lot of time and money if you already have that approval.

If not, what is the approval process, how long will it take and how much will it cost? Is it worth the investment? How likely are you and your product/service to pass? Do you meet the criteria and performance levels? Be certain on all these points before deciding to enter the market.

Sometimes this can be a far from straightforward process. The approval procedure may have been heavily influenced by local suppliers in their favour for example.

One company I worked with wanted to sell its products into Spain. There was no official Spanish approval or CE marking for their product, so on the face of it market entry should be easy. Unfortunately, no!

Spanish manufacturers had found a local way to have a CE marking on their product, even though an official

European harmonisation procedure had not been agreed. They then successfully lobbied for this to become a requirement in contracts, effectively keeping out foreign competition unless they managed to find a way to achieve CE marking too!

Secondly, is there a trade body you need to be a member of? Is membership open or closed and what is the application process? Again, look at the costs versus potential returns. In some countries it can be the case, or at least common practice, that a particular product/service is only bought from members of the relevant association. I came across this in Germany recently for one client for example.

Next, we need to look at the competition. Not to be afraid of them, but to be aware. The existence of competition shows there is a market, but we need to be aware of their strengths and weaknesses. This will also show us what other barriers we need to overcome.

How strong is the local competition? What market share do they have? What is their value proposition? Do we offer any technical, quality or value benefits?

Market share can be bought, but is it worth it in the long run? The effect can be to drive the whole market down and start a price war. That can only affect margins and benefits the customers most of all. It is usually best to sell the value of your product or service: the outcome rather than the price.

Other barriers to entry that need to be considered are customs duty and arrangements; transport costs and availability. Will freight and duty costs make us uncompetitive? Can we reliably deliver on time?

Is language going to be a barrier? Is English commonly spoken in business? You can overcome language issues with local staff or representation, but there is a cost which needs to be considered.

Look at all the possible barriers to market entry, make a list, identify the threat level of each and your ability to overcome them. Assess whether market entry is feasible given these obstacles.

I use a simple template with the most common barriers to entry already listed, space for your assessment, and a scoring method which will help you evaluate the market viability. Each barrier to entry is given an importance weighting in order to calculate a score for each country. This allows scores to be compared and a priority list of countries to be collated. See Section Consolidate & Rate below for the template.

Currency

How are you going to sell in the target market?

Will you demand your home currency? If so, how will this affect sales? It may mean that the real price locally of your product/service varies with exchange rates.

This can work either way, to your advantage or detriment. It is best to factor this into your decision-making process. Consider your margins and what level of currency fluctuation you can absorb, or price variation the market can stand.

Is your currency readily available in the target market? Can you accept an internationally recognised trade currency such as $USD or €Euro?

This can be a real limitation on the growth of your business if you are not prepared. It is an ever-changing situation which needs to be evaluated and acted upon.

For example, I worked hard with one company to open a market in Nigeria. We accepted payments in $USD which was the usual trading currency. All was going well until oil prices tanked and the availability of the currency became difficult. Payments out of the country were restricted by the Government and so, consequently, was the customer's ability to buy.

It is important to weigh up this risk and your exposure, don't get caught out with money outstanding and a lack of currency available to pay you.

Is it feasible to accept the local currency as payment? Again, we need to consider the effect of possible fluctuations in exchange rate. Also, will your bank accept the currency and convert it? What will be the charges? How competitive will the rate be?

If not, do you set up a local bank account? This is not always as straightforward as it sounds. You may need to have a legal entity in the country first. You also need to consider how you will get the money out of the country again. What are the restrictions, the legal and tax implications?

Currency can make or break a market entry, so be clear what you are taking on from the beginning and your acceptable level of risk. Speak to your bank, Speak to foreign exchange specialists, take professional advice. Be prepared.

Country Risk

Everything is looking good. We can overcome the barriers to entry and feel the target market is worth pursuing. Before we do however, take a step back for a moment and consider the country risk; the political and economic factors which are out of your control, but which can make or break your success.

How politically stable is the target country? Is the regime likely to change? How stable has it been in the past? How tight is the regimes control, are there signs of public unrest?

Sometimes it is hard to tell, but the effect on your business can be profound. I helped an Indian company to open a good market for their products in Libya under the Colonel Gaddafi regime. At the time he seemed to have a strong hold over the nation and regime change seemed a remote possibility….then came the so-called Arab Spring!

Cemex, the Mexican cement producer, invested heavily in Venezuela, only to have their plants nationalised by Hugo Chavez with no agreement on price. Eventually they were offered about half of their estimated value.

Even in the so-called developed nations of the West there can be risk of political change. Look at the tariffs introduced by Mr. Trump in the U.S.A. and the decision of the U.K. to leave the European Union. We still do not know the full effect on trade of that one!

Be aware of the economic situation in the country also. Is the economy growing or shrinking? Investigate the strength of the banks and their liquidity situation. If accepting payment by bank Letter of Credit, be certain that the issuing bank is solid, if not ask your bank to add their confirmation i.e. guarantee of the payment. There will be a fee for this, but it is worth it for the peace of mind.

In the end of the day it comes down to assessing the likely risk of entering your target market and limiting your exposure. Be aware of your organisations attitude to and ability to withstand risk and act accordingly.

My intention is not to put you off, exporting can be greatly rewarding, it's just best to go into it with open eyes and a great deal of awareness.

How politically and economically stable is the target country? Is the regime likely to change? What is the likelihood that international sanctions or tariffs are applied? Is the economy growing or shrinking? Do the banks have any liquidity issues or concerns?

How comfortable do you feel about the risk?

Consolidate & Rate

If you've been following the series of emails and gathered the information suggested, then by now you will have a lot to consider. Each piece is a part of the puzzle and needs putting in its place in order to decide whether to continue in our programme.

When we carry out this process on behalf of clients we consolidate all of the above information into our specially designed template to weigh up the pros and cons, the potential versus the risk.

It looks at each element and gives it a rating or a score, then calculates a final rating/score taking in to account the weighting of the most important factors for you in your business.

This gives us an overall rating/score interpreted from **'prime target'** to **'do not touch'** as a guideline on which to base a decision on the viability of the target market, or a comparison of several potential targets.

7 Steps to Export Success and Export Brokering

Selection Factor	Rating Matrix	Rating 1-5	Weighting	Score
Market Size	1 = Low, 5 = High	4	20%	0.8
Growth Rate	1 = Low, 5 = High	3	5%	0.15
Barriers to Entry:				
Approvals/Registration	1 = Difficult, 5 = Already Hold	5		
Competition	1 = Strong, 5 = Light	3		
Transport	1 = High Cost, 5 = Low Cost	4		
Language	1 = Strong Barrier, 5 = No Barrier	5		
Currency	1 = Difficult, 5 = No Issue	4		
Payment Terms	1 = Not Manageable, 5 = Acceptable	3		
Customs Duty	1 = High Cost, 5 = Zero Cost	5		
Total B2E		29	50%	14.5
Product Adaptation to Market	1 = Needs a lot of work, 5 = Ready to Go	5	10%	0.5
Brand Awareness	1 = None, 5 = High	1	5%	0.05
Country Risk	1 = High, 5 = V. Low	5	10%	0.5
			Total Score	16.5

STEP 3 – HOW?

We've now identified the **Where**, which is our target market. Next, we need to focus on the **HOW**.

How are we going to reach the market? How will we carve out a market share? What will be our route to market strategy?

The first important factor is to **FOCUS**. STEP TWO may well have identified more than one potential market. Our Resources Checklist in STEP ONE will have helped us to recognise the current capabilities of our organisation. Referring back to that, we need to decide if we can effectively focus on one or more than one market at the same time.

Is your organisation ready to deal with more than one country, language, packaging, paperwork, customs regulations, number of additional customers, stock etc?

Do you have the people available to follow through on your plans? It will be counterproductive to try to enter more than one market only to find you cannot cope with the extra work and start letting clients in all markets down. This can and will affect your whole business!

Focus is key in gaining market entry. Spread yourself and your resources too thinly and you end up scraping the surface and never really getting under the skin of the market itself.

This is a recipe for failure. Focus your efforts on where you assess the best returns will be available based on the resources at your disposal.

For the purposes of the remainder of this chapter, we will assume you have decided to focus on one market, which is a sensible initial approach.

Others can follow on later, sometimes very quickly. It just depends on your success in entering the first market, resources and your attitude to risk.

First it is important to say that we must focus. STEP 2 may have identified more than one potential target market, but we need to decide which one, or how many we can effectively target at one time. Focus is key in gaining market entry. Spread yourself and your resources too thinly and you end up scraping the surface and never really getting under the skin of the market itself.

That is a sure-fire route to failure. So, focus your efforts on where you assess the best returns will be available.

Once the focus is defined, next we must explore the options for gaining market entry.

Distributors and Agents

Is the best option to work with a local distributor or agent? This is a low risk strategy on the face of it, with little fixed cost, but to offset that is the risk of lower returns.

What is the difference between a Distributor and an Agent? Apologies for going over this if you already know the distinction, but for those who are new to exporting there are important differences which need to be carefully considered.

A **Distributor** is a local company that will buy your product, market and sell it themselves. You rely on them to generate the leads and secure new business.

They are your customer in the target market. In fact, if you enter in to an exclusive agreement, they will be your only customer! You invoice them, they invoice the end user and take the corresponding credit risk.

Sounds simple right? Well yes and no. As with anything there are plusses and minuses to this kind of arrangement.

An **Agent** works very much in the same way in terms of promoting your product in the market, with the exception that they are working on your behalf, and it is you that will invoice the end customer, paying them a commission for their efforts. Think of an agent as a commission only sales person for your company.

So, what are the plusses and minuses of each option? Let's look at it from each stage of the sales process.

From a marketing perspective there is a subtle difference. A distributor may well have a strong name in the market, which will quickly help you to gain market awareness and confidence in your product/service. Market entry can be quicker and penetration deeper due to the distributor's connections.

On the other hand, your identity and brand can become lost, with the distributor the stronger presence. The customer is used to dealing with them, you may not have a direct relationship at all. What happens if you decide to change distributor or they opt to drop your product? You could be back virtually to square one.

An agent should be able to offer the same connections to the market and introductions to the customers. In this case however as you are invoicing the customer, it is you they become used to dealing with, you have the contacts and greater control over the process.

With this benefit comes a minus however. It is you that takes on the payment risk, assuming you are offering credit. A distributor is taking on this burden and making credit decisions based on history with the customer, local practice etc.

A distributor may also overcome the currency issue too, as you can sell to them in your home currency, and they can sell to the customer in the local currency.

On the other hand, you have all your credit eggs in one basket with a distributor and may well have a greater overall exposure.

So, which is the best option I hear you ask? The answer is it depends! It depends on what type of product or service you are offering for one thing.

If you manufacture small components, electrical for example, you may well be better to use a powerful distributor such as RS Components in the U.K. They have the name, the sales outlets and pulling power to the customers. They can offer you the expectation of volume which may well be more important to you than promoting your brand.

If, however, you offer a technical product or service which requires a lot of input from your team to make a proposal, define the scope and install the system, then to a large extent it is your expertise, your name and experience which the customer will be buying. In this instance it may be preferable to have an agent whose role is to open doors, make introductions and ease the process.

This is particularly true if the value of the project is high, and the payment terms based on project milestones for example.

As we have seen, the decision between agent and distributor is not always clear cut. There are subtle yet important differences. There are also legal distinctions, which vary country to country. Be certain you know the implications of whichever option you choose.

Whichever way you decide, the next critical factor is choosing the right distributor or agent. Get this wrong and it can severely disrupt your progress in the market.

Do not rush in, take your time to assess potential candidates, talk to more than one. Visit them, get a feel for the company, who their customers are. Do they really specialise in your market sector?

From the initial work we did in STEP TWO did any names keep coming up? Is there a stand-out candidate company you would really like to get on board?

Ask around. Check with potential customers if they would recommend anyone. Look at the exhibitors or delegates at recent or future conferences. Check the advertisers in relevant magazines or journals. Look at the members of any relevant trade association. Do a web search. Ask for support from the Commercial section of your embassy in the country.

In short, look at all possible avenues to create a target list of names to contact and explore. Approach them with details of your product or service and shorten the list to those who show the most interest, combined with required market presence and potential.

It is very important to choose carefully. This distributor or agent will be the face of your company in the market. You may well be judged by who you are associated with. Make sure they have a good solid reputation and a long-standing interest in your market.

Also look at their existing portfolio of products or services. Who do they already represent? Are they complimentary or competing? Are they operating in the right market sector? Do they appear to have a lot of products already for the resources at their disposal? Is this a concern?

A well-connected representative can be worth their weight in gold in helping you make entry into the market. With the right connections they can fastrack you in front of the right customers, but beware those who promise amazing things when in reality they are either already fully committed, not in the right market space or have conflicts of interest.

It is not unheard of for a supplier to be tied up for years with a distributor/agent who either cannot, or deliberately does not, market it aggressively. Be wary of those who profess to be well connected or related to the Prince or Government Minister.

Once you have narrowed it down to one or two potential companies, suggest a loose working relationship to start with until you are both sure you are a good fit. See if they produce the goods, open the right doors and hopefully secure some orders before rushing in to an exclusive or long-term contract.

Remember making the right choice is critical to the success of your market entry strategy.

Recruitment

We've looked at the upsides and downsides of distributors and agents, plus how to select the best ones. But is this the best option for your business? Would you be better to recruit your own sales person or people? What should you consider in making that decision?

There is no doubt that there is greater initial risk and commitment, at least financially, to recruit your own people in the country. You have the task and cost of recruiting the right person, their salary and other fixed costs to bear for a period of time before you actually see the returns.

Inevitably it will take them time to settle in, to be trained, to contact the right potential customers and secure the first orders. How long this takes will depend on their background, whether they have knowledge of the market already, not to mention their personal drive and determination.

One way to speed up the process is to look at recruiting someone from a competitor. Someone already therefore in the market and with existing contacts. Invariably such a person will demand a higher salary and benefits than someone new to the market due to the additional value they can bring, so it is important to determine that they really have the influence they say they have and that the customers respect them.

Even if they do, it is not guaranteed customers will change suppliers just because the sales person has moved to you. There are often many factors at play in the decision-making process. That said, this is a good place to start to explore the possibility of recruitment and to gauge the salary levels.

Recruiting the right person from a competitor, with knowledge and experience in your market, can lead to fast results and a seamless market entry, however. They will be able to advise you what is required to break into the market and levels of price/service required for example.

It is also important to consider the challenges of employing someone remote from your main office. Have you done this before? Do you have the expertise to manage remotely? Can you trust them to perform when you are not present? How do you keep on top of the situation? Reporting structure etc.

There may well also be legal and tax issues to be clarified and it is strongly recommended you take local legal advice before proceeding. There are different regulations on employment contracts for example, different tax implications and employee rights. You may need a legal entity in the country to employ people for example.

From experience, even within the EU the rules and regulations are different. One client had employees in France, Germany, the Netherlands and Portugal. Each one required a different set up and legal contract.

Distributor versus Recruit?

We know there is greater risk in employing someone. There is more of a financial commitment initially due to their fixed costs.

What about the returns? What is the breakeven between using a distributor/agent and employment?

A distributor/agent is paid by commission, the level of this will vary depending on the margins and volumes in your product, so each situation is different. Let's take an example:

The distributor/agent for Product A will receive a commission of 25% on all sales.

The total cost of recruiting someone will be say €100,000 per year including all taxes and benefits.

On sales of €100,000, commission cost is €25,000, whilst employment cost is €100,000.

The breakeven point is €400,000 sales.

At this point, the costs of the distributor/agent and the employee are the same.

Anything above €400,000 then it is more cost-effective to have your own person. At our target of €1m of sales, you will be saving €150,000 by having you own person.

It's a simple calculation, combine that with how long you think it will take to reach each level of sales in each scenario, to then calculate the investment required and period you will be exposed to risk.

Does that fit with your self-assessment in STEP ONE? Is it affordable? Will the effectiveness of having your own person outweigh the risk at the beginning?

This is an assessment which companies like Go Exporting can help you with. We have years of experience evaluating the different elements and reaching a conclusion based on sound reasoning and financial calculation.

Direct Sales

We've looked at the options for entering a market through local representation but should also consider if your product/service is suitable to be sold directly from your home country or via e-commerce.

Increasingly these days products are purchased online and shipped across borders. Will this work for you?

Generally speaking e-commerce is most effective for smaller, more consumer led products, though increasingly business will buy certain items online also. Where a product is more technical in nature or requires greater customer service, the sale is unlikely to be completed entirely online although 74% of all sales start with an online search. Google states that 57% of the purchasing decision has been made **before** the customer contacts you!

Think about the implications of that for a moment. Your website is critical. Ensuring customers find you and then find the information they require on your website is critical. Otherwise, you could be losing out big time! The importance of effective digital marketing has never been higher.

Generating enquiries and sales through your website is one of the great developments in the last 20 years. The website is your constant advert to the world about your company, product and services. It can also contain an e-commerce shop where customers can buy and pay for goods directly from you 24/7.

Just having an eye-catching, well-presented website and ecommerce shop is not enough however. Unless customers know where to look for you or how to find you, it's not going to do much. You need the support of a digital marketing expert to drive traffic to your site by optimising your results in search engines when customers search for the keywords related to your product or service.

It's an art to drive traffic to your site, combining not only SEO but also utilising social media to generate awareness and interest.

To those of us of a certain age it's a bit of a black art! To those in the know it's the only way to go. Uses the services of a specialist digital marketing company to maximise your reach. Click here for further details.

Time to Commit

We've reviewed the different options and calculated the investment required, compared that to our resource assessment and attitude to risk. Now it is time to commit to our preferred route to market option.

Once you've decided, do not waver, focus on it. Find the best distributor, agent or employee, whichever is your choice. Be patient. No need to take the first thing offered. Look around. Ask a lot of questions. Seek advice from people you trust within the market and within your company. Make the right decision.

Be certain that the investment required is both affordable and justified. Will the returns exceed the costs, do they warrant the exposure and the risk?

Are you comfortable with the predicted timescale and the time investment required from your current team? **Remember that a distributor/agent should actually be viewed as your most important customer.** They are often more work than an end customer. They need nurturing and supporting, motivating and enthusing about your company and products above all others in their portfolio.

At this stage of the process with our clients we pull everything together into a detailed plan. We recommend you do the same and would be pleased to support you in this process. Click here for details.

Define all the key elements and the objectives including:
- Required financial investment
- Required non-financial resources
- Timescale
- Level of Risk
- Route to Market Strategy
- Milestones along the way – what you need to achieve, by when, to be successful
- Expected Outcomes at each stage 3, 6, 12, 24 and 36 months

Make sure you are comfortable with the overall plan and the detail, with each of the elements above. Discuss it with your stakeholders to ensure everyone is on the same page. Obtaining the buy-in from colleagues now will save a lot of questions later on.

Review and compare the plan to the actual results often. Highlight any anomalies and work to put them right. Be vigilant in keeping the plan on track.

If it is working, great. If not however, do not be afraid to question everything. Are you delivering the resources and investment agreed in the plan? Is it the execution that is wrong or the plan itself? Don't be afraid to change tack if necessary but be sure of the reasons first.

7 Steps to Export Success And Export Brokering

STEP 4 – WHAT NOW?

We now have our target market and have developed a focussed strategy for the route to that market, with clear milestones to hit along the way.

We have now decided upon our target market and have developed a focussed strategy for the route to that market, with clear milestones to hit along the way.

Excellent, but how are we going to put the plan in to action? It's all well and good having the perfect strategy on paper, but it's no good if that's where it stays. Someone has to implement the actions, make sure we hit the milestones and reach our targets.

Do you have the internal resources, an Export Manager or Director for example? Do your staff have the skills and experience? Is everyone already busy with their existing roles and you do not want to jeopardise their success elsewhere?

Remember even if the strategy is to appoint a distributor or agent, you still need someone to lead this; to find, support and motivate the distributor, to make joint visits etc. A good representative should create more work and by that, I mean opportunities, for your organisation, not take it away.

If you have the skills and experience internally then this is usually the best option, providing always that the resource has the time to be able to concentrate on this target market.

Don't fall into the trap of spreading your people too thinly. To make a success of a target market requires focus; it requires time and energy to dig deep into the market to uncover opportunities, to fully understand the market dynamics, the competition etc.

Customers want to see a constant presence, not what I call **'touch and go selling'**, where you make a big effort for two weeks, a month, and then nothing for 3 months whilst your team is occupied elsewhere.

It is better to fully concentrate on one or two markets than to try to cover four, five or more with the same resource. One organisation I worked with actually had one Sales Manager covering 32 countries! Yet the same company had another Sales Manager who concentrated on one country, gained 70% market share, with the same turnover at better margins and lower costs than his colleague.

Both were excellent sales people, equally dedicated and knowledgeable, but the organisational strategy for one of them was wrong.

Expand only as quickly as your resources will allow you to focus on and fully implement the strategy in your target market.

What if you do not have the internal resource to implement the strategy? In this case one option is to utilise the services of a consultant or independent sales person. A good one, with the relevant international experience, drive and determination can be an excellent additional resource to your business.

They have the advantage of being flexible also. You can buy-in the amount of time and expertise required, with less commitment and fixed costs. This can be a real advantage if you are dipping your toe in the export pond for the first time and want to see the results before making a full commitment.

Choose wisely, however. Make sure the consultant has the skills required and the time to properly allocate to your project.

We will look at these options in more detail later, but for now whatever the decision it is important that the person(s) has the time to dedicate to the plan, to this new target market.

It takes time to fully understand a market, to know the movers and shakers, to dig deep and uncover opportunities. You cannot do that if your team is spread too thinly. Make sure they have the time to allocate to this important task.

Importantly customers want to see a constant presence. This builds confidence in your company and your long-term commitment to their market. Not all customers are looking for a quick, short term gain by constantly switching suppliers, they like to build relationships. Reliability is imperative to them.

You cannot build that customer confidence with 'touch and go' selling.

"A man's GOT to know his limitations" as Clint Eastwood famously said in the movie Magnum Force way back in 1973! It may be a generation ago, but the truest sayings stand the test of time.

Inside Resource?

Depending on the size of market you are targeting, the potential returns and your available resources, having someone dedicated to the new market within your organisation to lead the charge is usually the best option.

As we touched upon previously, it is important this person has the time to focus and the expertise to make a difference. Do you have a current member of staff with the experience and expertise in international markets? Do you have an Export Manager or Director for example? Will your current Sales Manager or Director cover both roles? Has he/she the time to do this effectively?

The last thing you want to do is to grow your export sales, but to damage your current sales at the same time by taking away time and resource. The net effect will end up being zero, or even worse, negative on the organisation as a whole.

It is not a given that, because someone is a star performer in their home market, they will be able to work to the same level internationally. It is not something you know instinctively how to do.

Assess their experience and expertise. Use an outside resource to do this if in any doubt. You may want to consider using a Mentor to guide them in the initial phases until they feel confident to go it alone.

They need to be aware of the way of doing business in your target market, to be flexible, and importantly to be patient. The fact you are market leader in your home country does not necessarily impress your targets. It may open doors, but you have to earn respect and trust in the marketplace. That all takes time.

Even if you're route-to-market decision was to look for a distributor/agent, as we have seen, you need an experienced internal resource to motivate and support, to ensure they are working tirelessly on your behalf.

It is not a given that an existing employee will want to take on the challenge. This role will require a lot of travelling, time away from their family and friends, often time alone far away from home. It's not for everyone.

If you do not already have the resource then recruiting someone new is the next option. Recruiting always has its challenges, are you actually getting what it says on the tin for example. It's expensive and you are definitely adding overhead to your business where it may take some time to generate a return.

If you find the right person however this can be the start of something good. They will have the time to dedicate to the new market, coupled with the right knowledge to make an impact.

So, look closely at your internal resources first and see if anyone fits the bill. If not, you have a decision to make; recruit the necessary expertise as a full-time employee; or as we will discuss in the next section, use the services of a suitably qualified and experienced consultant.

Outside Resource

After assessing your internal resource, you may have concluded that no one currently fits the bill for this new export role, to lead you in to the unknown new market. That's not unusual, after all you probably were not looking for the necessary skills and experience for exporting when you recruited your team.

You may also feel recruiting someone new is a risk and expensive at the same time. You may not want to increase your head count or fixed costs at the present time.

The option then is to utilise the services of a consultant with the necessary international sales experience. They can help create faster results as they know from experience what is required, who to talk to and how.

Their experience means they are aware of what to look for in a distributor or agent, how to generate the first customers and can advise you on making sure you are ready internally to fulfil the customer's expectations.

A good consultant with the necessary drive and determination can be an excellent resource for your business. You also have the benefit that it is a flexible resource. You buy-in just the amount of time and expertise as you require or your budget will allow. There is less commitment and fixed costs.

This can be a real advantage if you are dipping you toe in the export market for the first time and want to see the results before making a full commitment.

Comparing costs on a daily basis to having your own employee will on first glance look expensive, but remember you avoid the hidden costs of employing someone, the potential hassles and headaches.

The right consultant, with usually years of experience and expertise to draw upon, is a flexible resource that can bring fast returns, without you having to make a major commitment.

STEP 5 - PREPARE & GO

By now we have settled on our target market, decided upon a focussed strategy to enter that market and have decided who will implement it, but before we get ready and head off into the sunset (or more likely sunrise for an early morning flight!) we need to make sure everything is prepared internally.

Communication is the first key element. Make sure everyone, and I do mean everyone, in the organisation is aware you are about to embark on an adventure in a new market. Ensure they have the right information to deal with any questions or queries that may come their way.

There would be nothing worse than a potential client contacting your company only to be told by the receptionist, internal sales team, or whoever answers the call, that you do not sell to that country!

Next check that you have everything necessary prepared in the correct language and format for your target market. Do not just rely on English to get you by. It shows commitment and respect to your potential new customers to provide information in their own language.

Don't just rely on Google translate either, we recommend the services of a specialist translation company, click here for details.

Consider the following list of common items that require translation:

- website
- brochures
- advertising & other promotional material
- proposals/quotations
- technical documents
- product labels
- instructions
- health & safety information
- Terms & Conditions
- Order Forms
- Warranties etc

When collating your barriers to entry list for your target market did you find that local approval or registration was required? Have you put this in place? If not, how long will it take, and can this process run alongside your initial approaches in the market? In some countries it is necessary to have a local representative to actually complete the process for you. Sometimes this can be your distributor/agent if you have already decided upon one, but if not, there are often specialist agencies that fulfil this service on your behalf. They will know their way around the local officialdom, so can be an important ally.

Next ensure the logistics are in place to quickly and efficiently deliver your product to the customers once you receive the first orders. DO NOT leave this until later when you start receiving orders as by then it will be too late if there are any issues which need to be overcome. Do you have sufficient stock of the right products and do you need that to be held locally?

What about customs requirements? Paperwork such as Certificates of Origin? Duties? VAT etc? Do you know what you need to do for each scenario? Would you benefit from a bonded warehouse?

Logistics and Customs are a specialist area which we again recommend you take professional advice to prepare yourself and avoid any expensive pitfalls. This is especially true with the changes Brexit has brought for UK-EU trade.

Go through the entire sales and order process in detail to ensure you and your organisation are completely prepared to deliver your product or service to the customer.

"You only have one chance to make a great first impression". So, make sure you have done everything in your power to ensure you do!

Value Proposition

You've probably heard of USPs (Unique Selling Points) and probably have a pretty good idea of what these are for your product or service? As you are already successful in your home country I'd be surprised if this was not the case.

Be honest though, how unique are your Unique Selling Points? Do they really differentiate you from the competition?

I prefer to consider your **'Value Proposition'**. This looks at the equation from the opposite side i.e. from the customers perspective. In the end of the day they are going to buy, or not buy, depending on their perception of the value your product has for them.

In essence they will take each of your USPs and decide what their benefit or value is for them. It's not whether your products on/off switch is blue or green, but how important that is for them. If they are red/green colour blind like me, then the colour of the switch may have a high perceived value!

Your Value Proposition in this case if I was your target customer could be:

'Our blue on/off switch, as compared to the green used by our competitors, means even the red/green colour blind can clearly see when the unit is active, reducing risk of accidental injury.'

This is a deliberately simplistic example, but it serves to illustrate the thought process you should follow.

Think about your target client in the new international market. What is likely to be important for them? What are they looking to achieve, or what problem are they looking to solve, by purchasing your product or service?

Understand this and you can create desire and perceived value for your product by highlighting the key elements which deal with your customer's needs.

This is your Value Proposition.

This may be different in each country or target market, so think about it carefully before pressing ahead. Be clear what message you need to put forward to clients, how you are going to create desire and perceived value.

This will help you avoid merely competing on price, after all it is likely you will not be the cheapest in the market and, in most cases, you don't want to be either!

First Steps

We are ready to go, full of excitement and expectation of untold riches from this mystical new market! But where do you start? What now?

The first thing we do is to create a 'hit list' of the top 10 key players in the market who would use your type of product/service or could benefit from your new technology for example.

If your route-to-market strategy is to appoint a distributor/agent then identify 2-5 possible partners also.

These tasks are not mutually exclusive, even if you are looking for a distributor/agent, you should still compile a list of target customers. Often the best partners will be recommended by a customer. Remember, if they have proposed them, they are likely to be comfortable dealing with them, which will make your market entry easier.

How do you identify your hit list? There are many options, searching the internet is a goldmine of information these days. Be specific in your search phrase, such as 'car parts dealers in Germany' or 'alcoholic drinks distributors in Australia', whatever is relevant to your product/service.

You can also ask any existing contacts you have in the country for their opinion/help. Your Chamber of Commerce or Export support from your government may be able to help also. Contact the commercial section of your embassy in the target country too. Supporting business expansion is what they are there for after all.

Look at your customers in your home country or other export markets, do they have subsidiaries in your target country? Ask them for details and a referral. This kind of warm introduction will make your job a lot easier.

I used this approach to great effect to enter the Russian market with one company. From zero we went to $2m sales inside 2 years. This platform of warm contacts made market entry quicker, plus helped raise credibility even with the local companies once they learned we were dealing with their rivals.

Once you have your initial hit list start making approaches by email or telephone introducing your company and products. Plan these approaches carefully, make sure they are compelling and interesting, that they convey your Value Proposition and create a desire within your target customers/partners to learn more.

Include an immediate reason to act by suggesting an exploratory meeting and having some dates ready when you are planning to visit the country. This will focus their mind on whether your proposition is of interest now, rather than putting it to the backburner to be considered at a later date. Creating a sense of urgency leads to action.

Don't be afraid to be proactive in your follow up. If you've not heard anything from them after 2-3 days, send a reminder and a further call to action. Something like 'The schedule for my visit is filling up quickly, but I really want to meet with you as I believe there would be mutual benefits in working together. Can we agree a date for an introductory discussion?'.

This direct approach is the best way to take the first steps into the market before visiting. Once you have several meetings lined up it will be time to make that first visit to the country. This will be a learning curve, a fact-finding visit. You will gather a lot of information about the market, the movers and shakers, where you need to be to be successful.

Go with an open mind and a keen eye for sales opportunities!

Look for any forthcoming exhibitions, conferences or trade association meetings which you could attend. Beware spending too much on a speculative event however. Make sure it is targeted at your core business and will attract the right audience. Consider attending as a visitor/delegate initially to get a feel for the market and make contacts. Often the exhibitors themselves and organisers can be very helpful. Generally speaking at this stage, the direct approach will be more cost and time effective.

Be prepared for the meetings with the information you want to gather, get a feel for the market, ask potential customers who they would recommend as a distributor/agent, who else they think you should speak to. Build up your contact list and try to see as many people as possible. If its not possible to meet then make a date for a further visit.

On this visit and the next, be on the lookout for openings for the all important first trial orders. However small these are worth their weight in gold. More on that in STEP 6.

In the first 6 months it is important to be very visible in the market. Keep in contact and visit often with your hit list, but also expand on it, get your brand out there in the market, get people talking about you, especially the competition! Once the competition starts to notice, you know you are making headway and it actually lends credibility that they think you are worth being concerned about.

In STEP 3 – HOW? We drew up a plan with milestones and targets. Review that constantly to make sure you are on track. Securing those first orders is critical, momentum is key. I liken it to rolling a snowball downhill, it starts off small and slow, but gradually gets larger and increases speed, until it becomes an unstoppable force.

If you are looking for a distributor/agent you should by now have identified your preferred partner/representative. Don't rush in to a decision and give away exclusivity easily however. Look for their commitment, for evidence of the benefits they can bring, ideally a few customers and first orders. Take time to get to know them and their capabilities.

Marketing

Now you have taken your first steps into the market you may be contemplating a marketing campaign to coincide with your approaches and first visit. Whilst there is something to be said for this, I have consistently found the direct approach to be more worthwhile and cost-effective.

That said there are some effective and relatively low-cost ways you can get your name out there and set yourself/company up as an expert in your field.

First and foremost, make sure your website is prepared and available in the language of your target market. Yes, English is the business language, but generally customers will prefer to read in their own language. They will grasp the messages you are trying to convey, your Value Proposition, better in their mother tongue. For that reason, it is important to have a professional translation by a trained and qualified translator.

Use social media and digital marketing to announce your arrival and drive traffic to your website. Create a lead magnet, a white paper or article of interest to your target market which shows your expertise. Make sure this is available in the language of your target market!

This is a whole topic which could take up a book on its own. We recommend using an expert digital marketing service to support your efforts with regular tweets, blogs, building backlinks etc etc in order to build your online presence and accompany your launch.

Also find the relevant local trade magazines, local and national press, online news outlets, blogs, whatever publications may be relevant and send them a Press Release on your product/service now being available in their country. It's free and any articles published will enhance your presence and reputation.

Look out for forthcoming exhibitions, conferences or trade association meetings which you could attend. At this stage, depending on your budget, its ok to just visit the events, not to take an expensive stand for example. Walk the floor, network, make appointments beforehand from the delegate list or exhibitor profiles. Use the time wisely to meet the right people. The organisers will often be a great source of information for you and can make introductions to key players.

You will have plenty of approaches to spend your hard-earned money on advertising, directories, exhibition stands etc. Resist the urge to splash the cash initially until you are sure the expenditure will be worthwhile. In these early stages you are trying to gain a feel for the market and make contacts. Being proactive in your approaches will be more effective.

The Visit

Once you have a few planned meetings it is time to make that first all-important visit to your target market. It is important to plan this carefully and to allow time in your schedule to slot in other meetings/contacts that you unearth whilst in the country.

This first visit will be as much a fact-finding trip as a direct sales effort, although obviously sales are the ultimate objective! On this visit it is important you gain a feel for the market and the key players for example. Talk to as many people involved in your industry as possible, whether they could be direct customers or not. Make an appointment to see the relevant trade body, perhaps the government department, your countries local embassy commercial section.

Be well prepared for the meetings. Know who you are talking too, find out as much about them and their business as you can beforehand. LinkedIn is a great tool for this. It is important you appear knowledgeable and interested in them.

At the same time ask them lots of questions. Prepare in advance the information you want to gather and create a check-list for yourself to make sure you cover everything. That time in front of your contact is precious.

Remember however you have two ears and one mouth for a reason! Listen twice as much as you talk. Listen carefully to everything that is said, and not said during the meetings. Be attentive and aware. Pick up on the little things your contact says which may point you in the right direction as to what is important to him. Learn how you can tailor your Value Proposition to his needs. Picking up on the subtleties can be the difference between success and failure.

Always ask who else you should be talking to during your visit. Ask for their advice. Your contact will like to feel important and to appear well-connected. Ask who they would recommend as a distributor/agent if that is your preferred route to market. Build up your contact list and try to see as many people as possible during this visit. The evenings are also part of your working day on this trip. Use them by inviting contacts to dinner and drinks. You often find out a lot more this way! Not to mention often making good friendships which can last for years.

Don't ignore the younger, more junior people in the organisation either. You never know where they will end up. Being friendly and interested in them can be time well invested for the future. I became friends with a young, junior engineer in Egypt 15 years ago who within a few short years was head of department and then moved on to set up his own successful business. All through that time he made sure he included my company in any tenders and even when I changed industries has helped me find the right contacts.

Such contacts are truly invaluable, not to mention rewarding.

Whilst we have said this is very much an information gathering and introductory visit, be on the look-out for opportunities to secure trial orders. Ask the question 'Do you have any requirements at the moment where you could try out our product/service?'. Even a small order is a step in the right direction and can be worth their weight in gold. More on that in STEP 6.

Once you return home you will no doubt have a long list of things you promised to do for the people you met, whether that is sending extra information, samples, technical details, whatever you have said make sure you do it, quickly and efficiently. This is your first opportunity to show what a good company you are.

Always follow up, keep the contact going. Often you can have what appears to be a really positive meeting but then when you return home it's hard to get any response from the contact and things seem to stall. There can be many reasons for this, but don't be put off. Keep pressing, suggest a follow up conference call and dates for the next meeting.

In the first 6-12 months it is very important to be seen to be consistently visible in the market. Convince the customers you are there to stay and they can rely on you if they do decide to change suppliers. Avoid the 'touch and go' selling. Visit the country often. Make it your second home.

This will get your brand out in to the market, get people talking about you, even the competition! Once they are talking about you then you know they are concerned. This gives you credibility in the eyes of the customers.

Assess and Appoint

By now you will have visited your target market at least once and will be planning your next visits. You will have made a lot of contacts, gathered mountains of information and gained a real feel for the market, its key players, movers and shakers.

If you have not already secured your first orders, then now is the time to really push. Customers have seen you in the market, know what you can offer and your Value Proposition. Look to finalise some deals. There is no greater satisfaction than to start seeing the fruits of all this hard work.

It may be tempting, and you will certainly be asked, to give a special introductory price. Whilst this may seem tempting in order to secure some business, be wary that is does not set a precedent as the pricing expected in the market. It can be used as a stick to beat you with later as customers see the introductory price as really your best-selling price.

Better is to offer volume discounts or rebates. If they order more, then you can offer a better price. This can be done retrospectively too, so you set an annual volume level for example and agree that if they reach that level you will give x% rebate, but only when they have reached that level.

If really pushed and as a means to secure the first order you could offer the rebate in advance for the first order but make it clear that this volume then does not count towards the annual target or rebate.

If you are looking for a distributor/agent you should by now have narrowed down your search to the one(s) you would like to work with and who you feel will bring the best returns. Remember it's not who you like best, but what they can do for you which is the most important selection criteria.

Don't rush in to give away exclusivity to one company, unless you really are certain they are the best choice, and they can bring immediate results. For example, are they prepared to invest in stock and commit to minimum purchases throughout the year?

Look for their commitment, for evidence of the benefits they can bring. Do they have customers lined up ready to order? Take time to get to know them and their capabilities. Suggest an MOU (Memorandum of Understanding) as a way of getting the ball rolling prior to entering into a longer-term contract.

Once you are ready to commit to a contract ensure it is carefully drafted and does not conflict with local law in your target market. It is always best to insist that your home country legal system is the basis of the agreement and used to resolve any disputes, but you do need to ensure you are not in breach of local regulations also.

Build into the agreement the minimum term, sales targets, marketing responsibilities, break clauses and notice periods, a dispute resolution mechanism, credit agreement etc. This is a legal document which needs to secure your company, but also show commitment to the distributor/agent.

If you are working on an agency basis be particularly careful on the contract to ensure the agent does not become a quasi-employee under local law with rights should the arrangement end. Also ensure it is clear that any personal tax liabilities are their responsibility.

Distribution/agency contracts are a complex area and we recommend you take legal advice from a company with international business knowledge. Your local solicitor may well not have the expertise in this area.

Review

You are now well along the way of your export journey in the target market. You have made several visits, appointed a distributor/agent, secured the first orders and are ready to fly.

But are you where you thought you would be by this stage? How does your progress compare to the Milestones and Targets set in STEP 3?

Now is the time to go back and review. Compare where you are today compared to where you predicted you would be. Is it the same or similar? Are you way out?

If you are broadly on track then all well and good. It you are significantly behind schedule then it is time to review again your plans. There may well be good reasons for this, indeed your milestones could have been too optimistic in the first place, but you need to review internally to ensure everyone is on the same page and the support is there from the organisation.

The initial phases are always difficult. It can be very stop/start. You may feel you are making great progress one day, only for things to grind to a seeming halt the next, then something good happens and off we go again.

Take a step back and look at your overall progress. That is the most important point. Are you going in the right direction? Consider asking an outside expert to review your progress and your plans, make any adjustments necessary and set you off on the right road for the next stage of the journey.

Entering a new market is like rolling a snowball downhill. It starts off small and slow, gradually gets larger and increases speed, hits a few rocks which slow progress along the way, then speeds up and grows again, until it becomes an unstoppable force!

We are now at the end of STEP 5 and will start with the next stage in your export journey.

STEP 6 – PERFECT EXECUTION

Well done! You've made your entry into the market, created awareness of your company and product/service, secured the first orders and appointed distributor(s)/agent(s) if that was your strategy.

Job done right? Well, definitely **NOT JOB DONE!**

The real hard work is just beginning. Don't blow it now by being complacent or thinking everything will go fine. You have to make sure everything is perfect. First impressions really do count in this context. Make a mess of the first order and your job just became 10 times more difficult, perhaps even impossible.

Your new customer will be on the lookout for any problems, any errors, quality issues or lapses in service. They will already be slightly apprehensive about using a new supplier. You will be under the closest scrutiny and there may well be those in the organisation with long-standing relationships with your competitors who will be very resistant to change. Sometimes they can even be downright obstructive.

The key is to not give them any ammunition to fire at you. Make it perfect.

Ensure you are on top of the whole process from receipt of order, opening an account if applicable, delivering on time, logistics, paperwork, customs arrangements, packaging, user instructions etc. Make sure you have covered everything, give these orders your number 1 priority.

Make sure everyone in your organisation sees you doing this and engage them in the importance of these first orders. Make it a team effort, get everyone on-board with the importance of perfection.

It is important to make dealing with your company as straight forward as possible for your new customer, don't give them any reason to change their minds. **Close the door to buyer's remorse!**

Also critical is to ensure this first delivery, whether product or service, is the best quality it can be. Don't compromise or be tempted to 'make do' as this is a far-off market. Right now, it is your most important market! Get it right and it can become your core market of the future.

You'll never know if you don't do it right the first time and set the standard for what the customers can expect for the future.

Complete the Job

So, now we have delivered our first orders, we've ensured they ran seamlessly, it was easy for the customer and that the product/service was of the highest quality.

Finally, job done, and we can relax right? ***ABSOLUTELY NOT!***

This is just the start. In athletics terms, we are just off the starting blocks and about to explode up to full speed. It's taken a lot of time and effort to get to this stage, following the athletics theme, we've done the training and passed the preliminary rounds, we've started the race and now need to get up to full speed, then to finish strong!

Only in your business you will never reach the finish line as it will be continually moving further away, you will always be looking to reach new heights, to grow.

Don't make the cardinal error that a lot of new exporters make and think that your product/service will speak for itself and the customers will keep coming back. They don't.

Follow up with the customer, visit them soon after delivery, make sure they are happy with the product/service itself and that the whole ordering and delivery process has matched their expectations.

If there are any issues raised, however small or petty they may seem to you, deal with them, there and then, no delays or excuses, even if you do not fully agree with the assessment. Cut off the complaint at the ankles, don't let it grow to become a reason to go back to their previous supplier. Don't let the doubters in their organisation gain a voice.

If, despite your best efforts, there has been a genuine issue, that need not be a disaster providing you deal with it well. Sort out the issue, deal with it efficiently, compensate the customer if needs be, even a small gesture can often work wonders.

Provide all the support the customer needs and it can actually enhance your reputation in the future. Amazon has built an empire on this concept! Customer confidence is an important factor in deciding your success or failure.

In one company I worked with, we gained a first order for a key player in Germany for a highly engineered product which was critical to the operation of the customers production plant. Any issues would cost £1000's per hour in lost output. Delivery and installation had to be during their scheduled shutdown.

We were late delivering due to shipping delays. It was still within the shutdown, but the installation was going to run overtime. As you can imagine there were a lot of raised voices, tensions and blood pressure!

To resolve the situation, we flew in additional supervisors to allow 24/7 working and managed to finish just in time! We then provided an additional specialist process engineer to fine tune the system to ensure the customer maximised their output.

The result was the customer was happy and actually gained additional production capacity. The extra cost we incurred was paid back many times over in future business, not just with that plant, but with their whole group worldwide!

Always ask the customer "How could we improve next time?". This has a two-fold benefit. You are already building the expectation in the customer that there will be a next time, plus you will find out from their reaction their true feelings. If they say, "what next time?", then you know you have more work to do to find the root cause of their reluctance.

Always listen very carefully to what they say and what they do not say. Read between the lines. Ask others in the organisation too. Build a picture so you know what you are up against.

Then use the information to become their No. 1 supplier!

The Catapult

These first orders are your catapult to future sales. They are the basis upon which you will grow. As we have seen they are critical and require your 100% attention, before, during and after the sale.

What next? How do we turn the first orders into future orders and sustained growth?

The first easy step, but one which is often overlooked, is to never be afraid to ask for the next order! There's an old English saying "Don't ask, don't get" which is so true.

Find out how often your customer purchases your product/service. Know their demand and their ordering cycle. How far in advance do they order? Do they hold stock?

Make sure you are in the right place and the right time for the next orders. There's nothing more frustrating than calling a customer only to find they placed an order yesterday with your competition! Don't let that happen. Be in their minds at all times, know when to push, but don't be too pushy either to the point where you annoy them. It's important to build a good relationship with your customer, make them a friend even.

The next step in using the first orders as your catapult in the market is to ask, "Who else should I be talking to?".

You've worked hard to gain the trust of your customer and by now should have a pretty good relationship with key members of their team. Use that position to ask for their help. Generally, people like to please and will be only too happy to show this and their knowledge by giving you their contacts. Ask them for a personal introduction.

These warm introductions make your job of creating credibility and reliability that much easier. If Company X is using you then Company Y will feel that much more relaxed in making a buying decision.

Leverage these relationships to as great an extent as you can, and you will soon see business growing.

Next ask your contacts if it is ok to use their name when talking to other companies as a customer using your product/service. Usually they will say yes but be on the lookout for any potential conflicts and rivalries. Sometimes it can be counterproductive to say you sell to one company if the rivalry is high.

Ideally ask your customer to put something in writing showing that they are ordering from you and that they are completely happy with the product/service and support of your organisation. If they do not have time, offer to write it for them just to sign if they are happy with the content.

With their permission develop this into a case study to really highlight your capabilities. Show the benefits you have brought to the customer, really highlight your Value Proposition. Include quotes from the customer, photographs where relevant. Create a picture of how great it is to deal with you and the real, tangible benefits for the customer. Go in to as much detail as your customer will allow without giving away sensitive information.

References and case studies from key players in the market will quickly build your credibility and confidence in your organisation. Be systematic in your approach, make it part of the sales process, not an afterthought when asked by your marketing team.

There is no difference in approach when using a distributor/agent. You need to work with them to ensure they follow this approach. Insist on visiting the customer with them. As we have said before the distributor is in many ways your most important customer. At the same time, they are your primary sales point in the country, so use them to make sure you grow. Don't allow them to dictate the pace if it is slower than you want to go.

Follow these simple steps and you will see your business multiply. Keep pushing. Never relax. Visit the target market often. Keep your profile high. Show your intent to be a key player. Do this and the sales will come.

Before you know it, you will have achieved your target of £1m in Export Sales!

STEP 7 – GROW OR SLOW?

By now you are most likely 6-12 months in to your journey in the target market. You will have appointed a distributor/agent or your own sales person, gained the first customers, delivered the initial orders and the amount of repeat business will be growing.

Depending on your typical order value you will have that £1m sales target in sight in the coming months. Your reputation in the market will be enhanced and the opportunities opening up.

Everything on the surface is looking rosy. You are probably thinking about the next steps, maybe even considering a subsidiary or JV in the country.

STOP!

Take a step back for a moment. Remember those milestones and targets from STEP 3, have you checked them recently? Are you on track to where you hoped to be?

Are you actually making any money? Remember turnover is vanity, profit is sanity! Can you see a clear path to profitable business from where you are?

It is now time to reassess your strategy and planning. Look again at the risk versus rewards, at the resources of your organisation and what you can realistically achieve.

How fast do you want to grow? What will that entail in terms of investment, risk, resources? Which risks are you willing or able to take? Expanding in the market will undoubtedly expose you to further risk, whether it is cashflow, bad debt, stock requirements or people resources.

Develop a Stage 2 strategy with the key stakeholders in your organisation incorporating new milestones and targets. Analyse the returns versus the costs.

Decide whether to Grow faster or Go Slow towards your targets.

Do you have the right distributor/agent? Are your own people performing? What effect has the export drive had internally? On your home market?

There is a lot to consider in developing a stage 2 strategy. Using an outside consultant can help with this process to give unbiased opinions and advice based on years of experience.

Once you have developed your Stage 2 strategy, including new Milestones and Targets, discuss it internally with key stakeholders and again ensure the whole organisation is on the same page.

Move forward together at whatever pace you have decided is best for you.

Ready to FastTrack your export journey. Need some support?

For a no-obligation discussion on how
Go Exporting can support your export growth please call +44 800 689 1423 or
e-mail: info@goexporting.com.
All emails will be responded to personally within 24 hours.
Or click here to secure a **FREE CONSULTATION** with Mike Wilson our CEO.

Act quickly though as only 5 spots are available each month.

Foreword

"This is Bob Serling and I'm the creator of multiple products on licensing for generating direct sales and substantial passive revenue. Some of my courses include Million Dollar Licensing, Million Dollar Joint Ventures, and Ultimate Leverage Licensing.

As a marketing and licensing consultant, one of the marketing campaigns I became well known for got the name, "The 25$ Million Letter", due to the fact that my client landed an agreement for a $25 million project by sending it to just one client. However, while I was paid well to write that letter, I made exponentially more by customizing the letter for dozens of clients and licensing it to them for a fee and a royalty share.

Over the years, I've helped many well-known marketing experts increase their sales with licensing. Some of these experts include Roland Frasier, Ryan Deiss, Derek Gehl and Frank Kern. One of my most successful students is Ramzi Bouchrit who applied the licensing and joint venture strategies in the International Trade industry to connect professionals in this business to close 7 and 8-figure USD export deals. Many of his most successful deals involved partnering in exports of soy beans and timber from America and Africa to East Asia.

While most of my students applied my teachings in industries such as finance, marketing, web design, and business development with great success, doing this in the International Trade industry was a bit unconventional. This underscores that when joint venture and licensing principles are applied properly, it can lead to tremendous results in nearly any industry. And that's surely the case with Ramzi's application of these strategies in the Import/Export business.

I've been teaching licensing and joint venture strategies for more than 25 years and what Ramzi applied in his import/export business and explains in this book is what I call a Toll Gate Joint Venture. In Ramzi's case this starts by choosing the best importers, qualifying them based in their need, seriousness, and the longevity of the need to guarantee a project's profitability. It then proceeds to secure the payment for the exporter through successfully finalizing the deal by making sure each party involved in the deal gets its appropriate cut.

Brokering deals in the International Trade industry is about listening to your business partners, understanding their needs and providing solutions they couldn't create on their own. This is what differentiates the successful deal maker (JV broker in Export) from a simple introducer who focuses only on getting paid to connect an importer with an exporter, then leaving them both to continue the journey on their own.

International Trade is like any high-ticket industry that requires patience and focus. What's explained in this book helps the exporters and middlemen looking to build solid distribution networks overseas (importers & distributors) and grow their sales by learning the essential principles. By applying these principles, you'll add new income streams to your import/export business as you start considering the hidden and unseen opportunities around you and increase your profits. Ramzi includes many real-life examples of deals he brokered where everyone benefitted handsomely.

If you'd like to discover how you can monetize the unconverted deals (where you could not directly satisfy one of your importers needs), the hidden opportunities, and how to leverage the relationships you've built with your business partners in order to increase your final sales figures with no huge expenditure (in some cases with zero costs), this book will give you the JV brokering tools to do that."

WHY EXPORT?

WHAT IS EXPORT?

In a nutshell, exporting is the process of selling product(s) or services in foreign markets.

WHY EXPORT:

Foreign markets impose strong discipline on firms which encourage competition and efficiency of operations. Individuals/firms/companies of a nation engage in export trade in order to achieve the following objectives among others:

- ✓ To earn foreign exchange;
- ✓ To increase profit levels;
- ✓ To expand an existing business;
- ✓ To gain access to bigger more profitable markets
- ✓ To tap vast export potentials;

- ✓ To reap economies of large scale production;
- ✓ To exploit opportunities of new market;
- ✓ To support government export promotion and policies;
- ✓ To finance economic activities of the nation;
- ✓ To even-out cyclical fluctuations;
- ✓ Gain international esteem;

WHO IS AN EXPORTER?

An exporter is someone who sells goods or services in a foreign market(s) in order to make profit among other objectives. Exporters can be classified into the following categories:

1) **Manufacturing Exporter:** This is a company which apart from being manufacturer of a particular product or ranges of products, also exporting the same product(s) by itself, this could also include the farmers who produce a farm produce and export the products by themselves.

2) **Export Merchant:** This is an exporter, who buys goods/products from the manufacturers or farmers to

resell them to an overseas market (export),

3) **Export Agent / Brokers:** The agent /broker does not actually export but serves as a contactor between the overseas importer and the local/international exporter, such agents use their knowledge of the export products, the target market as a platform of contact between the overseas importer and the exporter. They receive commission for their service depending on many added values, from "finder's fee", "procurement fee". They're known also as Match/Deal Makers. Becoming an export broker is one of the easiest (but needs a high level of professionalism) and the most rewarding ways any prospecting exporter can raise money to go into full time export business. There are many ways of sourcing for foreign contacts/serious importers; the most common way is simply to use the power of common sense, recommendation, digital networking using the internet. With the internet you could scout for reputable foreign Consignee/Importers, and do due diligence check on them online. Another way is to make use of your friends and relations abroad. Once you locate foreign Consignee/Importers, your next step is to know their requirements and specifications. Armed with this knowledge, you can now proceed to look for local

producers that meet those specifications and connect the two parties for an agreed commission.

CHAINS OR CHANNELS OF EXPORTATION

Farmers and Growers of farm produce/Manufacturers: These people are the ones that make the actual growing of the crops for export/final products. Most of the times, they don't do the actual export directly but sell either directly to the exporters or to a local sourcing agent who sources independently or for a big export company.

Local Sourcing Agents from Farmers: These are people who source for product from local farmers/manufacturers. They usually have very good and close relationship with farmers/manufacturers and as such, they do this with very high advantage even in times when they have no money can still get things done and that is why some big exporters will always make use of their services. Beginner and/or Expert professionals, who either, lack or do not want to use their own funds, are usually found in this category as their knowledge is the only thing required here.

Exporters: These are people who are into the actual moving of goods out to the foreign countries to receive hard currencies in exchange.

Export forwarding Agent: After goods are procured by the exporters, depending on the distance to the port, they will either need to convey goods for trans-load into a container or load directly into a container to be taken to the port. Someone is usually in charge of preparing and making this happen effectively, and this is where the job of an export forwarding agent comes into hand.

METHODS OF PAYMENT

METHODS AND TOOLS OF PAYMENT IN EXPORTING

The process of exporting is incomplete without receipt of payment. Any business deal is considered complete, only if each party gets its share: the buyers receive what they paid for, the exporters get their full payments, and every party involved in the whole transaction too. Below is the most recognized method of payment in exporting:

1. Letter of credit aka L/C

2. Documentary Collection

3. Open Account

4. Consignment

5. Cash in Advance

1. Letter of Credit (L/C)

It's one of most safe methods of international. The **documentary credit** aka **letter of credit**: is an arrangement whereby the importer requests and instructs their issuing bank to pay the exporter (by releasing funds to their bank account) against delivering a pack of specific document(s) agreed in advance by both parties, provided that the terms and conditions of the documentary credit are fully complied with.

TYPES OF LETTERS OF CREDIT

Irrevocable Letter of Credit

A letter of credit (L/C) can be either: revocable or irrevocable. The Letter of Credit is deemed to be irrevocable in the absence of any indication. An **irrevocable letter of credit** cannot be amended or cancelled without the consent of the issuing bank, the confirming bank, if any and the beneficiary. The payment is guaranteed by the bank if the credit terms and conditions are fully met by the beneficiary. The words "**irrevocable documentary credit**" or "**irrevocable credit**" may be indicated in the L/C. In some cases, an irrevocable L/C received by the beneficiary may become invalid without its amendment or cancellation; this can be due for instance: when the bilateral transactions (import and export) between both countries are temporarily/totally suspended such as in a trade sanction, or when the issuing bank has ceased operation.

Revocable Letter of Credit

The **revocable letter of credit** (as it's clearly stated) gives, the issuing bank at any time without the consent of the beneficiary (the exporter), the possibility to amend or cancel it often at the request and on the instructions of the applicant (the importer). This means, the exporter has no security of payment in this type of letter of credit (L/C). The words "**this credit is subject to cancellation without notice**", "**revocable documentary credit**" or "**revocable credit**" usually is indicated in the L/C.

Confirmed Irrevocable Letter of Credit

The exporter who gets paid via this method of payment is assured of the payment even if the importer or the issuing bank defaults. The confirmed irrevocable L/C is particularly important from Consignee/Importers in a country which is economically or politically unstable. In a confirmed letter of credit, the exporter or the importer pays an extra charge called the **confirmation fee**, which may vary from bank to bank within a country. The fee usually is added to the exporter's account. The exporter may indicate in the sales contract that the confirmation fee and other charges outside the Exporter's country are on the Consignee/Importer's account.

Unconfirmed Irrevocable Letter of Credit

Unlike the **unconfirmed irrevocable letter of**

credit, the guarantee of payment comes from the issuing bank only.

Tips based on Real Life Examples we faced

When you enter an L/C deal, such as I like to call it when the importer will pay using a Letter of Credit, please make sure that you pass along all the needed information (not only documents) to your Bankers to help you issue first the draft, in addition to that you should take into account that it's just an instrument of payment, hence it's all about the negotiation first you set with your buyer, and based on what we've faced during our journey, this step should be done correctly, and since we can't cover all the possible scenarios, our advice is to seek the assistance of a professional financier in the LC (generally the financial department in your Bank HQ, or an Export consultant) to advise you in this step.

2. DOCUMENTARY COLLECTION

This is how it works: the exporter gives the collecting bank the instructions on what to do with the draft and shipping documents in what we call **collection letter** or **letter of instructions**. This letter states literally to the collecting bank the conditions under which the importer can receive the shipping and the actions to be undertaken.

DOCUMENTS AGAINST PAYMENT

In the **documents against payment** (D/P) --- **documents on payment** (**DOP** or **D/P**), aka **Cash Against Documents**, it's when the importer pays to receive the documents (bill and other documents) in order to obtain the products.

DOCUMENTS AGAINST ACCEPTANCE

While Documents against payment (aka Cash against documents) requires the importer to pay the amount of the draft at sight, Documents against acceptance requires payment by a specified date.

Tips based on Real Life Examples we faced

We had some deals previously between Nigerian and UAE (still do with a trustworthy buyer there) and he pays the exporters using the CAD method, in order to make it worthy and not risky for both parties, we used the service of a third party (as an escrow) logistics company based in Dubai to secure the funds and deliver it to the importer in exchange for the payment. My point here is in some cases you'll be faced with situations where you need the transaction (for whatever reason such penetrating a new market, good deal, etc.), so you need always to be sure that you closed all the wholes and minimised the pitfalls, plus make sure to have a plan B, C, etc. in order to close your deal properly.

3. OPEN ACCOUNT

In an **open account** trade arrangement, the products are shipped to the importer without guarantee of payment. Quite often, the importer does not pay on the agreed time. When you find yourself in situations like these, please seek protection using export insurance. Being in this business, please try always to be flexible, cautious and seek assistance from experts.

4. CASH IN ADVANCE (CID)

The cash in advance is considered the safest and preferred term of payment for the exporters. In some cases, the Cash In Advance is paid using the telegraphic transfer (T/T).

TERMS OF EXPORT PAYMENT

The terms of payment we covered above are:

- Bank transfer & Telegraphic Transfer (T/T)
- Cash against document/Documentary collection
- Cash against delivery
- Prepayment of a certain percentage of the contract value Any other type of payment agreed upon

Frequently and most commonly used for international trade

Terms of Payment (Method of Payment)	Terms of Trade (Method of Pricing)
This is the payment method used in an export transaction. It explains how and when the exporter gets his payment and can be as below: 1. Letter of credit LC 2. Documentary Collection **D/P and CAD** 3. Open Account 4. Consignment 5. Cash in Advance 6. Telegraphic Transfer T/T	This is the method of transaction for an export business. It explains on what terms will the pricing be made and can be as follows: 1. Free/Freight On Board FOB 2. Cost and Freight CNF, CFR or C&F 3. Cost Insurance and Freight CIF 4. Ex Works EXW

EXPORT TERMINOLOGIES

INTERNATIONAL COMMERCIAL TERMS (INCOTERMS)

The **INCOTERMS** (International Commercial Terms) is a universally recognized set of definitions of international trade terms, such as FOB, CFR and CIF, developed by the International Chamber of Commerce (ICC) in Paris, France. It defines the trade contract responsibilities and liabilities between Consignee/Importer and Exporter. It is invaluable and a cost-saving tool. The exporter and the importer need not undergo a lengthy negotiation about the conditions of each transaction. Once they have agreed on a commercial term like FOB, they can sell and buy at FOB without discussing who will be responsible for the freight, cargo insurance, and other costs and risks.

EXW {+ the named place} aka **Ex Works** title and risk pass to Consignee/Importer including payment of all transportation and insurance cost from the Exporter's door.

It's a multimodal incoterm,

In Ex Works the Ex means from.

Works means factory, mill or warehouse, which is the Exporter's premise.

EXW applies to goods available only at the Exporter's premises.

Consignee/Importer is responsible for loading the goods on truck or container at the Exporter's premises, and for the subsequent costs and risks.

In the quotation, indicate the named place (Exporter's premises) after the acronym EXW, for example **EXW Boston USA**. The term EXW is commonly used between the manufacturers (Exporter) and export-trader (Consignee/Importer), and the export-trader resells on other trade terms to the foreign Consignee/Importers.

Some manufacturers may use the term Ex Factory,

which means the same as Ex Works.

FCA {+ the named point of departure} aka **Free Carrier** All the responsibility of the exporters stops when they deliver the products to the carrier.

The exporter is obligated to load the products on the Importer's collecting vehicle; it is the obligation of the importer to receive the Exporter's arriving vehicle unloaded.

The delivery of products on truck, rail car or container at the specified point (depot) of departure, which is usually the Exporter's premises, or a named railroad station or a named cargo terminal or into the custody of the carrier, is handled by the exporter.

The responsibility of the importers starts as stated above (products delivered to the carrier) and they should pay the carriage/freight, cargo insurance and related costs and risks.

In the air shipment, technically speaking, goods placed in the custody of an air carrier are considered as delivery on board the plane.

Many importers and exporters still use currently

the term FOB in the air shipment.

In the export quotation, please indicate the point of departure (loading) after the incoterm **FCA**, for example **FCA Marseille France**.

FAS {+ the named port of origin} aka Free Alongside Ship

The responsibility of the importers starts, including payment of all transportation and insurance cost, once the products are delivered alongside ship by the exporters.

This incoterm is for deals where the goods are shipped via sea or inland waterway transportation.

The exporter is in charge of export clearance obligation.

The exporters should place the products in the dock shed or at the side of the ship, on the dock or lighter, within reach of its loading equipment so that they can be loaded aboard the ship, at Exporter's expense.

The importers are in charge of the loading fee, main carriage/freight, cargo insurance, and related costs and risks.

In the export quotation, please indicate the port of origin (loading) after the acronym FAS, for example **FAS Amsterdam Netherlands**.

FOB {+ the named port of origin} aka Free On Board

The responsibility of the importers starts, including payment of all transportation and insurance cost, once the products are delivered on board the ship by the Exporter.

It's used for products sent by sea or inland waterway transportation

CFR {+ the named port of destination} aka Cost and Freight

The responsibility of the importers starts, including title, risk and insurance cost, when the products are delivered by the exporters on board of the ship.

The exporters here pay the transportation cost to the destination port. We use this for deals by sea or inland waterway transportation.

CIF {+ the named port of destination} aka Cost,

Insurance and Freight

Same thing as **CFR,** add to it that the exporters pay the insurance cost to the destination port.

CPT {+ the named place of destination} aka Carriage Paid To

It's a multimodal incoterm.

The exporters are in charge of the delivery of the products to the named place of destination (discharge).

The Importers are in charge of the cargo insurance, import customs clearance, payment of customs duties and taxes, and related costs and risks.

In the export quotation, please indicate the place of destination (discharge) after the incoterm **CPT**, for example **CPT New York USA**.

CIP {+ the named place of destination} aka Carriage and Insurance Paid To

Same this as **CPT**, add to it the exporters pay the insurance costs to the named place of destination.

It's a multimodal incoterm.

The importers are in charge of the import customs clearance, payment of customs duties and taxes, and related costs and risks.

In the export quotation, please indicate the place of destination (discharge) after the incoterm **CIP**, for example **CIP Hong Kong**.

DAT {+ the named point of destination}

The exporters are in charge of bringing the products to and unloading them at terminal at the named port or place of destination

The destination point can be quay, warehouse, container yard or road, rail or air cargo terminal.

It's a multimodal incoterm.

In the export quotation, please indicate the point of destination (discharge) after the term **DAT**, for example **DAT Sacramento USA**.

DAP {+ the named place of destination} aka Delivered at Place

The exporters bear all the title, risk, responsibility involved to bring the products to the named place.

It's a multimodal incoterm.

DDP {+ the named point of destination} **aka Delivered Duty Paid**

The exporters are in charge of delivering the products to the importers to the named destination point cleared for import. The exporters should obtain the import license too.

It's a multimodal incoterm.

Delivered Duty Paid The Exporter is responsible for most of the expenses, which include the cargo insurance, import customs clearance, and payment of customs duties and taxes at the Consignee/Importer's end, and the delivery of goods to the final point at destination, which is often the project site or Consignee/Importer's premises. The Exporter may opt not to insure the goods at his/her own risks.

In the export quotation, please indicate the point of destination (discharge) after the term **DDP**, for example **DDP Lagos Nigeria**.

Export Documents

EXPORT CONTRACT

Understanding the main steps of the export transaction is crucial as it's basically always the same, and from my own point of view it should always start with "Finding the Distribution Channel" aka The Buyer/Importer of your products (your partner's products). The prospective importer might place an order for your products upon receiving your proposal/ letter of offer to supply the product in question. The order for your products by an importer is considered the start of "a firm EXPORT ORDER" and you as an exporter must ensure that it is genuine: meaning the issuer of the order is genuine, serious and financially able to pay on time the full amount of the transaction.

This Export order must be constituted by:

A sales contract for export must contain the following elements:

- Contract number
- Full name and address of the Importer and Exporter
- Name of product/ specifications
- The needed Quantity
- Packaging method and standard required by the Importer
- The agreed export price per unit.
- Destination (e.g. Tin can Island port)
- Point of delivery (e.g. Los Angeles port)
- Incoterm of sale (FOB, CIF, etc.)
- Method of payment (L/C, documentary collection, open account, etc.)
- The Delivery term (e.g. Cargo to be shipped 15 days upon confirmation of payment instrument for eg.)
- Name and signature of both parties: Exporter & Importer.

LETTER OF INTENT TO PURCHASE OR PURCHASE ORDER (LOI/PO)

A Consignee/Importer who is really eager to to buy a product from should quickly send to you *a Letter of Intent or Purchase Order* stating exactly what they want you to provide them, the quantity, the frequency of supply, the specifications and possibly when it is to kick off. I personally prefer to always use the filter of asking the importer to issue an LOI (if it's not already made) to see if they are proactive, from there I categorize the importers based on their replies. In a few words, if they prioritize and focus on satisfying their needs and are very responsive, that's the one major criterion for a very good business partner and with time you'll see it, since they will not waste time to move forward or say No from the beginning.

OFFER LETTER (SCO SOFT CORPORATE OFFER AND FCO FULL CORPORATE OFFER)

The Exporters issue the Importers this letter in response to the LOI previously issued by the importer spelling out in clear terms the availability of the product sought for, the quantity they can provide and deliver the price of sale, the technical specifications, the way of payment and additional clear information. At this step too, we could speak about a quote from the exporter to test his level of responsiveness and seriousness (same as the importer mentioned earlier), the aim here is to categorize you list of exporters too in a way to have a VIP list of sellers and buyers that you need to build deals based on that. With time, it will become a second nature and know from the beginning the entities that are the best fit to get introduced and connected together for very lucrative deals.

THE CONTRACT STEP

After the adjustment and agreement of the SCO/FCO between the Importer and Exporter, the final contract is issued biding both of them on the transaction they are about to initiate. Most of the deals we brokered and still do, it's rarely this step is done without our direct supervision (either our lawyers craft the contract or one of the business partners does it). Business transactions are very delicate especially if they take time such as the deals in the international trade, so many factors can emerge along the way and impact the transactions, so this written agreement once crafted well and written by experts who know most of the possible future scenarios will make all parties included abide by it and open to negotiate with time. That's the touch of a processional middleman/deal maker, and this is one of the reasons you should not play the role of a simple introducer in heavy deals (since most of the introducers are only after the small commission they get by introducing the buyer and seller then disappear to leave them on their own and in most cases it leads to disagreements or law suits).

HOW TO MAKE AN EXPORT CONTRACT ENFORCEABLE

HOW TO CRAFT WELL AN ENFORCEABLE SIGNED CONTRACT

It'd be advisable to refer to the case study below regarding the deals we've made while we had a law firm on board to protect each party, and please consult your legal advisor before any deal.

After negotiating the various steps of the international trade transaction, you need to put this under a written agreement, please do not underestimate this step, since it can turn either into a smooth business transaction or into a messy court fight.

Please focus on these steps to make a solid and enforceable contract:

1. Please Consult Your Legal Advisor Before Signing

Even if both parties took their time to reach the final version of the written contract, please do not take it for granted as it is what you think it is. Before you sign it, you should seek the assistance of your lawyer or legal advisor to be absolutely sure that you fully know and understand the terms of the document, in a few words: are these the final terms both parties agreed upon?

Once you sign a piece of paper (in some case even agree on an email content), the international law requires that you are bound by it. Unless you can prove that the other party did on purpose deceive in preparing the contract or inducing you to sign it, you will be required to abide by it.

2. Date of the Export Contract

Even if the export contract does not have to be dated in order to be valid and enforceable, it is recommendable to do so. Since the business transaction has deadlines: in producing, preparing, shipping the products, etc. dating a contract will help both of you to stick to these milestones. Hence, please make sure to state the milestones and their date (again: date of production, packing, loading, etc.), it helped us in all our deals we've done with our partners.

3. Please make Sure each party involved in the deal: Read, Understand & Sign the Contract

In some business transactions we've done where we met one of the parties: either the exporter or the importer, we made sure they take their time to read the contract, and then we ask them about its clauses to make sure they know and understand what they agree and sign on. This may seem like very simple (and it is!) but you'd be surprised at how helpful it is for all your deals.

4. Please make sure you negotiate and agree with the decision maker to sign the Contract

When you always start the discussion and negotiation, please make sure you deal always with a decision maker or their representative, ask the other party what is their position and role in the company. We've seen some deals fall apart because one of the decision makers (buyer and seller) was not involved in the negotiation in the first place; please always ask you need to be sure that the corporation is actually in existence, that the person signing on behalf of the corporation has the authority to do so and they're really genuine, and, that the contract was approved by the corporation's shareholders or directors.

5. Please keep track of all your Contracts

We've been involved in many deals where both parties disagreed at a certain point about one thing or more, hence once we remind them with the clauses and what they agreed upon, it was easy to settle down and move forward. That's why we make sure always that we keep a digital copy of the contract of each deal we supervise and broker in addition, we keep updating our partners via emails about any small adjustments, update, amendments, etc.. they both agreed upon even after signing the contract (if the email is considered as a legal proof in your country.

6. Please consider contracts signed electronically

Nowadays, many deals are closed remotely, and one of them took us 5 to 6 months in negotiation with the buyer until we reached to a final agreement and signed it electronically. Please consult always your legal advisor as this depends from a country to another.

Export Brokering Tips

How to get paid and from who

There are different models to get paid: the best one I found it suitable is an upfront procurement fee known as finder's fee, in addition to the commission per sales.

Basically it's selling the ready deal to an exporter(s) who is/are ready to execute the contract, these fees will cover your efforts done in order to look and qualify the whole transaction (the buyer, the price, way of payment, etc):

- Is the buyer is registered entity in their country?

- Is it a worthy and reasonable deal for any exporter?

Since in some cases you will find an import deal where the buyer is looking to pay a very low price for the products, or in some cases it's not a sought after destination for most of the exporters.

We also mean by a worthy and reasonable deal when there is no long daisy chains, meaning that are not many entities in the middle. Again you need to be in direct/close contact with the final decision makers.

In addition to the upfront procurement fees, you will get a commission for any shipment or sent goods from the seller to the buyer.

Meaning in this case you will get paid an upfront fee from the exporter for selling to them the contract and you can replicate this with various exporters if the contracts or the buyer/the importer is looking for huge quantities that cannot fulfilled by one single exporter.

Also you can get paid by the two parties, i.e.: the importer and the exporter.

You will get from the exporter as explained above the upfront fees and the commissions, and you will receive from the importer some fees when they are ready to pay you (some importers are willing to do so once they're in a hurry to receive the goods or they find difficulties to find suitable exporters so they are open to pay the broker who helps them in their needs).

How to secure our fees and which means to use

First of all you need to write everything down between you and the other party either the buyer (importer) or the seller (exporter).

This will be known as memorandum of understanding aka MOU, when you write everything down between both parties you will avoid any misunderstandings.

When you use the MOU or the memorandum of understanding, please literally:
- State the name of the entities or the signing parties,

- The date of start and when it ends,
- What are the goods,
- The amount to be paid when and how,
- Also it should include some NDA clauses or non-disclosing agreements clauses,
- And in case of a delay of payment from the other party what should happen,
- Is there a kind of extra fees to be paid, any penalties or any requirements that should be literally stated?

You should literally get assisted by a legal advisor before any deal as the laws are very different from country to another.

If you agree with the seller to be paid commission on each delivered containers or package, it is good you state it in the MOU, please arrange to get paid upon a specific number of shipments rather than a period of time. Here's why:

- In some cases the goods won't be delivered on time and in other cases the delivery can be postponed/cancelled for a period of time, so that's why you'd rather get paid based on the number of

shipped containers/goods rather than a period of time.
- Please arrange things with the seller in order to find the suitable number of shipments that suits both of you: you and the exporter

Please work hard to understand how generally things work legally in the country of the exporter, to secure your earnings.

In some countries signing your memorandum of understanding (MOU) between parties, the exporter and you in a local Chamber of commerce is recommended and can protect your earnings.

In other cases signing it in the embassy or the consulate can help you make it a very solid contract and cannot be breached.

In very huge deals where your earnings are very high, it would be better if you bring on board your law firm attorney or your legal advisor to be a partner in the deal (please negotiate with them a percentage or a cut of your final earnings), since this will motivate them and make them work hard to protect your earnings (theirs and yours) and avoid any legal pitfalls that would jeopardize your efforts.

Please operate with an international law firm that operate or handle international deals and it should be a member in any international and associations or law firms group that will generally give them the kind of reputation that makes them the best partner (legal expert that will do their best to work in your best interests).

What to look for and avoid in any deal (mostly it's about the business partners):

- Any good business transaction needs a bare minimum of transparency, prompt communication and respect of what all parties agreed upon... If for whatever reason you feel you're dealing with a non clear partner (either buyers or sellers) this for sure will cause problems sooner or later...

- Asking the right questions at the right time to the right persons makes the transaction goes smoothly.

- The best transactions start when you're discussing directly with the end parties & decision makers (end buyers and end sellers). Hence, please try always to broker deals this way unless one of the parties specifically stated or asked you to literally negotiate with their appointed official representative.

- Also be sure what's the final signing entity will be (the final buying and selling parties)... knowing who's going to sign the final purchase order or agreement will be crucial for your job and to know who's legally involved in the transaction.

- Please always write down a plan of action for any business transaction: plan every step from the start (when there's a need for goods) to the end (when everyone received what they asked for), this way will help you to anticipate all the possible scenarios and have a clear vision of the outcome of each deal/step. Generally once you apply this, you'll minimize from the beginning the last minutes surprises/decisions, also many unclear situations will become visible to you. It's literally like having the idea to build a house and by drawing a 2/3 D plan for it by a professional architect, it will become clearer than if it remained a simple idea in your head.

- Once you find a good and trustworthy partner, that's an important step, please connect or introduce them only to serious compatible entities by this way you show your professionalism and respect to all your business partners.

Please act as the protector for both parties interests (their time, their money, etc...) by this way, you gained the trust of all parties that worked and will work with you. Your credibility lies on this factor.

- Always start with the buying party since from there starts any business transaction

The biggest the need is, the higher chances you have to get a huge deal

- It'd be better to focus your efforts/start with goods and regions you have the best knowledge about. This will help you establish certain credibility in the market/industry.

For example, you may focus on certain industrial countries and see what they frequently import as raw materials for the daily operations of their factories, then you can dig deeper (through chambers of commerce, embassies, digital networking) to find importers, then understand their preferred products, the preferred import prices, and every piece of information that will help you to be very thorough and knowledgeable when negotiating/discussing with potential suppliers..

Your minimum task is to be sure that the end parties are legally registered in their countries, and they are really doing what they say

- Develop your own network of serious exporters and categorize them based on the A,B,C or 1,2,3 levels and same to the buyers to A,B,C or 1,2,3 levels, as well the brokers to A,B,C or 1,2,3 levels where the ABC or 1 2 3 levels (or more) is the system you're using to classify your business partners based on various professional criteria like: their responsiveness, their trustworthiness, their transparency, your own objective opinion also please do not forget to develop some relationships with debt recovery agencies, lawyers, freight forwarders and any professionals or experts that you will need their services in your future business transactions

Real Life Case Studies

How to leverage your network of local importers and increase your bottom sales with no extra costs:

We have an importer from United Arab Emirates who has his own list of importers based in Turkey, he imports from West Africa then he re-exports some of the products to Turkey at a higher price, the process were very profitable in terms of financial figures, but takes times, administrative documentations and procedure.

Since the relationship was & still strong with our UAE business partner (that's always our motto to increase everyone's final profits), we negotiated his final cut and suggested that we export directly to his final client based in Turkey and pay him his share.

The process was very smooth and we documented what we agreed on in a memorandum of understanding and we started shipping to Turkey.

How we've done it step by step:

- We've noticed that our UAE buyer was in need of huge number of containers on a monthly basis (15-30 per month from Nigeria),

- We took our time until the relationship became more solid: we were negotiating on his behalf deals with Nigerian exporters and we were doing a great job, since we were (and still use it until today) using the video technology to document the whole process of production, packaging of the products and loading in the containers.. That in itself made us work with a selective list of decent exporters and the importer was very satisfied since he's sure that we were looking after his interest, the same idea with the exporters.

- We are always close to our business partners and keep asking questions about how to improve the transaction process and increase the final financial figures (less headaches and more profits), that's where our UAE buyer informed us about the fact that some of the imported products are exported again to his buyers based in Turkey and since the original quality were already satisfactory (thanks to the trust built with them), we saw the hidden opportunity.

- We made a business proposal that he'll get paid directly his share of profits (the same figure), and our exporters will do the shipping directly to Turkey. By this way, he'll do less work and make the same profits. In a few words, we studied the whole scenario, figures, efforts, etc.. Then offered our UAE business partner (gate keeper in this case to his Turkish importers) a better scenario that will improve his business and it was accepted.

- The products were Charcoal from Nigeria to UAE & later directly to Turkey, around 10-15 monthly containers (20-22 Metric Ton per container) @450 USD per MT

Our UAE business partner earned a net share with less efforts, the final buyers in Turkey got their products quicker & directly from the source (West Africa), and our exporters gained access to a new base of buyers overseas, simply by leveraging our network and choosing the right partners who trusted us and made them feel and see that in the written agreement between all parties: exporters, UAE business partner, and the end importers in Turkey

Timber deals to Vietnam

50-60 monthly containers to Vietnam of Doussie wood (a specific timber available in West Africa that is needed in the furniture products made in China & Vietnam) @14-15k USD per container.

This deal was a bit delicate for us, since first the volume needed required that we either bring on board different exporters or take our time and find one single big Nigerian exporter to seal the deal, and secondly that the broker cut was a bit big (25-30 k USD per month since we set it to be, with any exporter, 500$ per container as net brokering fees).

We moved with the second scenario (one single big supplier from Nigeria) and they did accept to execute the deal without paying us any upfront fees to procure them the contract.

Step by step:

- We asked our network to recommend us some solid exporters who have a minimum of 5 years experience with a track record; in exchange our introducer will get a final cut of our profit.

- We've chosen one company that did already bigger deals (80 to 100 containers monthly to the same destination Vietnam), meaning they do know well the industry, they do have the financial capacity, they do have their own saw mills to process the products, above all, they know very well the importing country.

- We managed to meet physically the owners of the company and discuss with them all the details and document everything in a solid contract.

- To make it a solid deal and reassure every participant (buyer & seller), we managed to bring on board a very decent law firm based in Nigeria that offers also debt collection services with partners based in Vietnam (to execute a deep due diligence about the buyer and negotiate solid terms that put the buyer and seller on the safe side).

- We negotiated with the law firm to represent us and get 20% of our earnings (recurring), in a way that they will look after their and our cuts, aka contingency basis.
- We used as usual the video recording technology to make the buyer comfortable about the production process. What's amazing about this strategy is we also (as deal maker of the deal) managed to supervise the quality as well.
- Once all is put correctly, everything went well.

We gained in this deal; the expertise to use the contingency basis to bring on board a legal advisor and make them help properly & benefit financially, this is very advisable only when having a huge deal in terms of financial profits and delicate steps. Once I emailed the law firm I studied the 2 scenarios of how much the firm will make in case they simply prepared the contract and billed us by the hour or in case they'll be involved and gets 20% of how much we'll make especially they do have a presence in Vietnam, meaning always please make it more obvious in your partners' eyes how your proposal is more beneficial to them, that what makes the difference, and tells you that you deal with a smart partner.

How to adapt quickly according to circumstances:

PPE deal to Italy was one of my preferred successful deals (in my personal judgment) since it had many sides.

By the end 2019 we were doing very well with the timber deals and by that time Corona hit China and things (for those who remember) were very chaotic and impacted everything.

The tremendous needs for the PPE (personal protective equipments) increased and by February/March 2020 we've seen various factories in China stop their normal production and start trading in the PPE: such as Mask, Gels, Gloves, protective clothes, goggles, and related products and it was mandatory to make some new business partners in this line.

Step by step:

- February 2020, one of our business partners based in Europe sent to me a big urgent need for PPE in Italy (out of respect, please let me say a regional governmental agency was seeking huge and urgent supply to their hospitals as the situation at the time was very critical).

- Right away, I contacted some of my close business friends in UK & US who were involved in the industry to recommend me reliable ones. At the time, many offers were available, in order to tell the serious entities able to supply from the other ones, was quite time consuming in circumstances like that.

- I was introduced to a trading company based in the US that ships the needed PPE directly from China, they had already proven track record.

- The deal was very smooth

Wanted to insert this case study to emphasize on the facts that being proactive, leveraging your network and your humanity (care about others when doing your job) should always be your main tools in any business transactions.

Frankly, the financial profits were not very high in addition that was the only deal in PPE we got involved in, but it's the deal that strengthens my relationship with Mike Wilson (co-author) since his company was one of the business entities I sought help from, and with time I consider him a very trustworthy partner when it comes to deals with the UK. To emphasise on the idea I always believe in: your network is your net worth, please select them carefully and take care of them.

Soya bean deals to China

To progress in the business, we decided to play in bigger deals (8 figures in USD), we wanted to focus more on the Chinese needs since it's a big producing country & we started to focus on the Non Genetically Modified (Non GMO) Soya Beans since it's basically traded in very huge quantities (monthly 12500 MT deals, minimum & for 12 months as a start) for 430 USD per MT (deal in July 2021).

7 Steps to Export Success And Export Brokering

Step by step:

- I used the LinkedIn features to find some serious importers of soya beans in China
- I've chosen the best entities based on their reputation, history, their list of connections, way of posting, their comments, their partners comments, used Google to get the max of information about them, etc... This is helpful to know better your importers.
- There are also some well known Business Information providers: they do sell reports about any registered business entity worldwide (they can make a fresh investigation about it if it's not already in their database), and with these info you can decide either to deal or not with your current/new business partner.
- Some of the best quality non GMO soybeans around the globe is from Brazil, and it was our first time to deal with Brazilian exporters, in addition we did not have at the time "eyes" on ground, we sought help from the logistics companies in our network to connect us with their trustworthy colleagues based in Brazil to secure this part

(inspection, secure the payment, etc...), it didn't take time until we found the right agency there.

- Once a few importers were selected, we aimed to finalize with 2-3 firm orders that our list of trusted exporters can secure),

- The logistics company based in Brazil accepted the role & the offered percentage from the profits.

- They've helped us to settle down with the final exporters. The hard part was about how & when to connect directly the importers with the exporters, since the buyers required getting directly in touch with their suppliers, leaving us in a risky position.

The issue for me is how can we justify in the mind of both parties (since it's the first time we deal with the buyer and seller) that our presence in the deal is mandatory and goes beyond introducing/connecting them to each others, in general I personally do not get involved in fields where my company or my direct partners do not have any sort of control.

This is why we opted to have the logistics company in Brazil to act on behalf of the buyer in terms of inspection of the harvest of Soya Beans (the buyer required it to be max 1 year old harvest), in addition to the regular documentations, that was our window: we strategized the steps in advance, measured the risks of each party if we're not involved and supervising the steps of the transaction(the biggest reason of the Unconverted export/import deals is the negotiations since each party sees the whole transaction from their own angle which is always not objective), the fact that we presented to the buyer and seller what they asked & we were very responsive gained their trust and put them at ease to see us as "playmaker" of the deal, then things became easier.

Metals

This industry is very big and industrial companies in China (this is where our company is more focused and building a network) have huge needs concerning lead ore & copper ore.

Step By Step:

Currently, we are working on a few huge deals (monthly 1000 to 5000 MT in average) to some melting factories in China.

The above are cargos deals, where:

- The lead ore varies at the time of the deals between 1.8 & 2k USD per tonne
- The cooper ore varies at the time between 9-9.4 k USD per tonne.

The characteristics of these products are traded on a metal stock where the purity is the important criteria to determine the final price.

My point is: you should always aim the big deals (once you master the blueprint/process) and choose to deal with solid entities that are very keen to progress, this will push you to get better in your business skills (negotiation, closing, communication, etc ..) in daily use until they become a second nature.

Brokering huge deals has a flip side which is risking to invest one of your most non refundable assets: your time, so please do not consider brokering high-ticket deals as your "Lottery Ticket" where you close one transaction that will make you very rich, on the contrary, please treat it as a long term business, so please strategize, write everything down, keep records, make analysis of your blueprint, surround yourself with the experts in their fields (experts you need in your brokering business), and always keep on learning as it's the most important investment you'll make and see immediate results.

Our point in this book is to put the light on the huge potentials available in this business, there are plenty of companies out there in different countries that are looking for serious and long term suppliers

How to choose the right ones, that's the major question and to answer that, we've developed this book and you may refer again to the solutions above.

Any business, needs lots of caring about everyone's interests (not only our own), Brokering in international trade is no different and like I always say to my business partners: "we're our partners Dad" in a way to remind our self of our role to look after their interest and fill the gaps with the right elements to do a successful job, as simple as that.

Please do not take unnecessary risks for the only sake of chasing huge financial figures that you've predicted the moment you received a potential import/purchase order, there's only one solid path to make those figures a tangible reality, which is by:
- First taking care of yourself and that you're really in this deal to serve well and do what you promised others to do, and
- Commit to the success of the project.

Once you stick to these rules, the partners in this project (that you personally have chosen) will see and feel your dedication and this will lead to the dedication of the whole group to make your plan work, hence it becomes a matter of time until you really touch those financial figures, in addition to gaining your inner self esteem and respect that will make potential business partners run towards you saying: "we'd love to work with you because we are sure that our business and our interests are safe once you're around".

Some of the deals we've built during the last years were stopped due to some bans that happened in Nigeria related to ban in export of Charcoal & wood from there, meaning that it's always advisable to have a local consulting agency to give you some advices about the changes in the local laws that might impact your business and your progress, that's the case of Mike Wilson (the co-author) where he can advise you deeply about the Brexit and its impact on your international trade business to know what to avoid and what to do.

Thank You

I want to personally thank deeply every human being who has helped me to make this work that I hope to be of added value to humanity.

My partner in this book, Mike Wilson, who's very dedicated to this project, and who has put his expertise gained along the years to serve your needs.

My mentors who taught me about using the Internet Marketing and Joint Venture/Deal Making skills, especially Bob Serling who taught me well the principles of Joint Venture and how to broker high ticket deals was very kind to provide the above foreword and I strongly advise you to find a successful mentor in strategic partnerships (aka Joint Venture or Deal Making) and learn from them, this will make you ahead of your time and sought after.

Leif Holmvall from ExportPro.com and the Author of Export & Import: Winning in the Global Market, where he's one of the "Go-To" Export consultants.

My beloved family and business friends who made all my tasks easier, we enjoyed our work and get paid by helping other entrepreneurs resolve their need and gain their trusts.

And to you all: our readers, to trust us and shared with us our journey.

Printed in Great Britain
by Amazon